Obtaining Bible Promises
A Different Approach
for Every Promise

by
Dr. Roy H. Hicks

Harrison House
Tulsa, Oklahoma

Unless otherwise indicated, all Scripture quotations are taken from the *King James Version* of the Bible.

Some Scripture quotations are taken from *The Amplified Bible.* Copyright © 1965 by Zondervan Publishing Co., Grand Rapids, Michigan

4th Printing
Over 18,000 in print

Obtaining Bible Promises
A Different Approach for Every Promise
ISBN 0-89274-426-X
Copyright © 1986 by Roy H. Hicks
P. O. Box 4113
San Marcos, California 92069

Published by Harrison House, Inc.
P. O. Box 35035
Tulsa, Oklahoma 74153

Contents

INTRODUCTION

To write a foreword for this book is to say I do far more than agree with the teaching in the book. I am saying that the teaching is something I believe to be essential if the Church is to minister to the saints in the power it once did — something sorely needed in these last days.

Obtaining Bible Promises is a straightforward, clear teaching pointing out the areas we Christians have missed in receiving answers to our prayers by simply not understanding that different rules apply for receiving different promises.

Our experiences in life teach that different rules apply to different situations. When our children are small, we sometimes let them "bend the rules" to win games, but as they grow older and mature, we adjust and teach them the rules they must follow in order to win. Each game has its own set of rules. Playing one game and using the rules for another game simply won't work.

So it is with obtaining Bible promises. Each promise calls for a different approach for receiving it. Space would not allow for every promise — perhaps your favorite one — to be treated here. But I believe the guidelines presented in this book by my husband will illuminate some truths that will revolutionize your prayer life.

— Margaret Hicks

1
RULES: WHEN TO PRAY TO GOD OUR FATHER

The key or rule to when to pray to God the Father was touched upon in an earlier book by the author, *Keys of the Kingdom*.[1] In this book, the subject is amplified and some simple rules revealed for going to the Father, to Jesus, and to the Holy Spirit.

But when ye pray, use not vain repetitions, as the heathen do: for they think that they shall be heard for their much speaking.

Be not ye therefore like unto them: for your Father knoweth what things ye have need of, before ye ask him.

After this manner therefore pray ye: Our Father which art in heaven, Hallowed be thy name.

Thy kingdom come. Thy will be done in earth, as it is in heaven.

Give us this day our daily bread.

And forgive us our debts, as we forgive our debtors.

And lead us not into temptation, but deliver us from evil: For thine is the kingdom, and the power, and the glory, for ever. Amen.

For if ye forgive men their trespasses, your heavenly Father will also forgive you:

But if ye forgive not men their trespasses, neither will your Father forgive your trespasses.

Matthew 6:7-15

Most Bible scholars and commentators believe that Jesus was teaching the principle of going to His (and our) Father more than He was teaching that this prayer should be repeated, word for word, each Sunday in our churches. Isn't it interesting that Jesus warned against vain repetitions just before teaching how to come to the Father? Yet, in many churches this same prayer is repeated over and over, in many instances losing its significance.

In all kinds of churches, including Pentecostal, those who pray fail many times to ask the Father "in Jesus' name." John 14:13 says, **And whatsoever ye shall ask in my name, that will I do, that the Father may be glorified in the Son.** In the next verse, Jesus made His directive even stronger: **If ye shall ask any thing in my name, I will do it.**

I am not suggesting that the next time you're in a church service where this prayer is repeated you should stand up and shout, "God didn't hear us because we didn't pray in Jesus' name." But you might give the pastor this book and invite him to read this chapter, if you feel led to do so.

Some people may say it is not important to end a prayer with the name of Jesus, that it amounts to a technicality. Actually, however, the Lord's Prayer was given to the disciples, and there is no record that Jesus ever prayed it again. If God only goes by our hearts and not by scriptures that teach technicalities and principles, then it wouldn't matter to whom, or how, that we prayed, because He sees our hearts. Extending that thought to its logical conclusion, then would it matter whether we prayed to Allah in Mohammed's name? God *does* see the heart, but He has given specific and important guidelines for prayer, and we should, by all means, obey them.

I believe that not only does God expect us to use His principles of prayer but that not using them may be one reason many of our prayers go unanswered.

In a previous book, *Praying Beyond God's Ability,*[2] I quoted Dr. Raymond Cox as saying that Christians are content with a small percentage of answers to a large volume of prayer. When the millions of prayers that are prayed each day by millions of people of all faiths are counted, it is possible that less than 1 percent of them are answered. At any rate, the percentage is extremely low, I believe.

Jesus warned His disciples to be very careful not to become as the heathen with vain repetitions. He then made it clear that the Father knows what we need before we ask Him. After saying this, He went on to teach them the principles of praying to the Father. He did this, however, after a complaint from the disciples.

In Luke 11:1, they reminded Jesus that John had taught his disciples to pray, yet He had not taught them. So He proceeded to teach them how to pray. The principles of the Lord's Prayer are taught in detail in *Keys of the Kingdom*, so I will not repeat them here. I invite you to get a copy of that book and study the principles of worship and petition.

Please remember that any time you go to the Father for a need of any kind, you go to Him in the name of His Son, Jesus Christ. He made it very clear that we can go to the Father in His name, and we will receive what we ask. Especially note John 15:16, **Whatsoever ye shall ask of the Father** *in my name*, **he may give it you.** If He taught this to His disciples, we know that it holds true for us.

After teaching us to approach the Father in humility and worship, Jesus mentions daily bread, forgiveness, and deliverance from evil or the evil one. As worship is first, it follows naturally that we are to seek to ever be in His will. The will of God is always *good*, *gracious*, and *glorious*. To be in His will constantly will eliminate much of our petitioning because, in His will, we constantly receive all that we need. As we receive, we know it is because Jesus took our sins and gave us His righteousness. This is ultimate and supreme *graciousness*. Being constantly aware of it makes daily living *glorious* indeed.

Strive always to be ever in His will while here on earth. Many godly men believe that when you are out of God's perfect will, there is no divine protection by the angels or God. You are an accident waiting to happen or a potential victim of a sickness waiting to attack your body or mind.

When Jesus mentions our asking for "daily" bread, He was speaking of more than a day's provision at a time. This Greek word *epiousios* is used only in the Lord's Prayer. This word is not found in any Greek writings before it appeared in Matthew and Luke in connection with this prayer, according to Adam Clarke's commentary.[3]

Most Greek scholars agree that the word has a connotation of more than daily bread as we think of it. They believe it carries a strong meaning for our souls as well. It also carries a strong connotation of carrying over to the next day. As we ask for our daily bread, we are asking the Father, in Jesus' name, to please be aware that we need more than earthly bread for one day. We need enough to last us, body and soul, well into tomorrow in case we don't get to ask for it soon enough as the new day begins! By praying this way, we will have the residue from yesterday left over to begin the new day. Hallelujah!

Remember, also, that Jesus is *that bread come down from heaven*, so eat of Him through fellowship and worship.

Our prayer to the Father about evil, or the evil one, simply means our hearts cry out to be holy and to live a separated, sanctified life, to be free from Satan's will. Our desire is to live *out from under the things of the world* as Paul teaches in his epistles, or, as John teaches, *loving not the world neither the things of the world*. (1 John 2:15.) These are both good daily prayers and should be prayed from the heart.

The last thought that Jesus mentions is a daily walking in forgiveness. The word *debt* in the Lord's Prayer as recorded in Matthew 6:12 is referring to sins and trespasses. *The Amplified Bible* puts it that forgiveness means **given up resentment against.** How we need to search out hearts daily about this big word, *forgiveness*. It is so important, so vital, that if we fail to forgive others, then our own sins can not be forgiven.

When we don't forgive, we clutch our resentment to us. By that act of resenting, we cancel our own forgiveness, and sin is imputed to us again. Jesus paid *our* debt of sin. We are now in debt to Him to forgive our debtors. Lack of forgiveness on our part simply means we have no forgiveness and are, thus, a sinner. This daily prayer and heart searching is to keep us from resentment and unforgiveness and to help us to be sweet.

Resentment carries not only unforgiveness but is one of the leading causes of psychosomatic illnesses. Unforgiveness has the potential of causing all manner of sickness and suffering. This subject also has been treated at length in *Keys of the Kingdom*.

Please remember that, when you don't forgive someone, you are allowing them to give you *their* problem and now it has become *your* problem. A very big problem. But be forgiving. Go out of your way to forgive. Search your heart to see if there is anyone you need to forgive. God is the only One Who knows if you have truly forgiven or just put it out of your conscious mind. Seek God and ask Him to bring people out of the dim past, if there are any, whom you need to forgive. God will heed your prayer and bring their names back to you so that you can, once and for all, forgive them.

A Guide for Going to the Father

1. I always go to Him in the name of Jesus Christ, the Lord Jesus Christ, Holy Child Jesus, or Jesus of Nazareth.

2. I always worship Him first.

3. I ask Him to help me:
Be in His will.
Receive a supply of Heaven's daily bread.
Be free from evil and the evil one.
Forgive others.

Do I need a better job or a better car or a better education or better housing? I do not go to Jesus for these. I go to the Father in His precious name.

4. I do not forget to pray "thy Kingdom come" and to be concerned more about His Kingdom than earthly kingdoms.

This great subject of the rules that apply when going to the Father are well taught in the Lord's Prayer. I get to go to God, my Father, for anything and everything that I need in this life to make me happy. Of course, we know that what we ask must be in His will. Those of us who are parents know we cannot give our children all or everything for which they ask. Especially, when they begin asking for things that go beyond what they are mature enough to handle. God, our Father, has the same paternal yearnings and protective feeling for us. He cannot give us that which would harm us or make a contribution to our pride. We want our children to be happy and joyful, and we get to ask God for those things which will make us happy.

Don't go to Jesus in prayer when you should go to the Father, in His name. After studying this great subject, I believe our prayers that are prayed with so little thought must insult the Trinity. As mature Christians, we ought to learn the principles and apply them.

An Example of Prayer to the Father

Father, in the name of Jesus, Your Son, I worship You and give thanks to You for all blessings. I now know how to approach You and for what I am to ask. I believe You love me very much because I love Jesus very much. (John 16:27.) I am not afraid to come to You for all of my needs and for anything that will make me happy. I will be asking You in confidence, hope, and faith. I thank You now, in advance, for all that I will receive. Amen.

---

[1] Roy H. Hicks, *Keys of the Kingdom* (Tulsa: Harrison House, 1984).

[2] Roy H. Hicks, *Praying Beyond God's Ability* (Tulsa: Harrison House, 1977).

[3] Clarke, Adam, *Commentary on the Entire Bible* (Grand Rapids: Baker Books, 1967).

2
RULES: WHEN TO PRAY IN JESUS' NAME

The rules for going to the Father are easily understood. Principles regarding rules for going to the Father are clear and simple. Children going to their earthly fathers have no difficulty understanding this principle. We can go to our heavenly Father with the very same confidence with which our children come to us for the things they need and the things that make them happy. But church tradition may make it difficult for many people to understand why we should go to Jesus, instead of the Father, for some things. The rules for going to Jesus also are identified easily, but are very different.

Jesus Is the Head of the Church

When the owners or a board of trustees or the voters appoint or elect a head or boss or president, then he is the one to approach for any request that comes under his authority. You don't, by any stretch of the imagination, go over his head to the trustee or to those who appointed him. You go to the one in authority for those things under his jurisdiction.

And hath put all things under his feet, and gave him to be the head over all things to the church,

15

Which is his body, the fulness of him that filleth all in all.

Ephesians 1:22,23

God, our Father, owns the world and all that is in it, including the Church. The Church is His family. He has delegated the authority over the Church, however, to His Son. Jesus is the Head of the Church, made up of all born-again believers. The Body cannot live without the Head which signals and controls all of its functions.

If your body decided to go its own way and do its own thing, it would not only cause division but end up in chaos and confusion, even death. It is easy to see why there are so many factions, quarrels, and splits in the Church. People are acting apart from directions from the Head, Jesus. Our Lord is never a part of confusion. Where strife and trouble exist, **there is confusion and every evil work** (James 3:16). God is not the author of confusion. (1 Cor. 14:33.)

Apart from Jesus, the Church has no intelligence of its own, no spiritual intelligence and direction. One can see a picture of what is happening in the Church by looking at the innumerable masses of people who act apart from intelligence in giving in to their physical bodies' desires and appetites, ignoring their heads and better judgment. Our physical bodies only want one thing — to have all of their desires met at any cost. A child will pick up a cigarette, puff, and then begin to cough. Someone drinking an alcoholic beverage for the first time usually will gag and spit it out. As time goes on, ignoring all of the warnings and the intelligence of his head, he will go ahead and become addicted to life-killing habits. A good example is extreme obesity. Unless it is glandular, it indicates someone is ignoring their head, the seat of intelligence.

Jesus is our head and is ever desiring to become completely involved, as our leader, in every facet of our lives. After many years of serving the Church, I am continually shocked by pastors who will conduct service after service without consulting the Head of the Church, Jesus. So many churches operate by tradition rather than instructions from the Head. His Body shouldn't so much as set the time of day for the assembly to meet, decide to go to multiple services, plan the order of service, or spend money without consulting the Head of the Church.

Pastors should not structure the services, any of them, without praying about each and every detail of that hour. I have heard pastors say they would never have multiple Sunday morning services because they didn't like to have the congregation divided. They wanted to minister to everyone all at once, or they didn't enjoy speaking twice on Sunday. The pastor (as part of the Body) should not make a decision of that nature without consulting the Head, who is the intelligence of the Body. Yet it is done constantly.

How long do we worship? How long do we speak? When do we anoint and minister to the sick? These are all vital decisions to be made. How we make them will cause the Body to grow or fall away.

Jesus is the Head of the Church. If you are saved, He is your Head, your complete source for spiritual intelligence and direction. Do we, as individuals, always consult our Lord Jesus on vital decisions to be made? Seldom, in many cases. I don't advocate the extremes of some individuals I have heard about, such as not getting out of bed in the morning, not eating meals, not paying bills, etc., without seeking guidance. But I strongly advocate that you should consult Him for any decision that may affect your spiritual life.

Also, there are some purchases, some things you need that can cause you to suffer if you make the wrong decision. Without asking the Lord, you can end up paying too much for a luxury, for example, or buying such an expensive home that your budget is cramped and you have difficulty giving to the Lord. He should be consulted before you make any material decision that could affect you spiritually. Going to Jesus as your Head is the first rule to follow.

We Are to Do Everything in His Name

It is not a rule to *ask or consult* Him for everything. It is a rule that we are *commanded to do* everything in His name.

1. We gather together in His name. (Matt. 18:20.)

2. We are commanded to lay hands on the sick in His name. (Mark 16:18.)

3. We are commanded to cast out demons in His name. (Mark 16:17.)

4. We are to speak with new tongues in His name. (Mark 16:17.)

5. We are to baptize believers in His name. (Acts 2:38.)

(As a special suggestion to pastors, when believers are being baptized by immersion, baptize them in the name of the Father, Son, and Holy Spirit as scripture directs, then say, as you put them under the water, "and this I do in the name of Jesus." Thus you have obeyed in doing all things in His name.)

6. We are to command lame people to walk in His name. (Acts 3:6.)

7. We are to speak boldly in His name. (Acts 9:29.)

8. We are to speak peace by His name. (Acts 10:36.)

9. We may be called on to hazard our lives for His name. (Acts 15:36.)

10. We are to preach repentance toward God and faith to our Lord Jesus in His name. (Acts 20:21.)

11. We are to confess His name. (Rom. 10:9.)

12. We are to call upon His name. (1 Cor. 1:2.)

13. We are to give thanks in His name. (Eph. 5:20.)

14. We are to do all things in His name. (Col. 3:17.)

And whatsoever ye do in word or deed, do all in the name of the Lord Jesus, giving thanks to God and the Father by him.

Colossians 3:17

His name is mentioned so many, many times that to put them all down would be to rewrite the Bible. Just do all in His name: Give in His name, love in His name, forgive in His name, repent in His name, go to church in His name, worship in His name, witness in His name, and, above all, pray to the Father in His name. Please do not forget that one!

Go to Jesus Directly

Traditionally, we have gone to the Father for most everything we need. Listen to the average public prayer in church, and it will always be to the Father in Jesus' name. Perhaps 75 percent of the time, that is correct. But why is it that we seldom, if ever, hear of petitions going to Jesus? Why is it that the verse in John 14:12-14 is virtually ignored? Is it because we do not really believe the words of Jesus when He said, "Anything you ask in My name *I will do*"? He did say that. He did mean it. He has invited us to come to Him. Notice the context in which He said this. It is a context of the *sick being healed, blind eyes being opened, the lame being made to walk, and demons being cast out.* What He did while on earth, we are to do by using His name, involving Him.

Why can we not believe Him? It is because our traditions have superceded (and become) our doctrine. Do we have the scriptural authority to ask God to heal when Jesus taught us that He would personally do it that the Father might be glorified in the Son. (John 14:13.) If God does it Himself, then who will get the glory? Jesus wants to partner with us and bring glory to God, the Father, through signs, wonders, and miracles.

In the Great Commission (Mark 16:15-18), Jesus again confirms this by commanding us to go forth in His name and work these mighty works and miracles.

Recently, I heard some elders in a healing service asking God, as they anointed with oil, to heal in Jesus' name. Would it not have been more scriptural to command the sickness to leave in the powerful and mighty name of Jesus, as the disciples did in the Book of Acts? Notice that they used a compound form of His name, such as Jesus Christ of Nazareth, the Lord Jesus, the Holy Child Jesus, etc.

There are those who will point out that they were healed when they were anointed and the prayer addressed to the Father. This can happen because Matthew 18:19 says that if two believers agree on earth on any one thing that they ask, it shall be done for them by the Father which is in Heaven. (Matt. 18:19.) Any sickness would be a "thing," and when you find a prayer partner who will agree with you, the sickness will have to go.

Prayer

Jesus, please help me to personally partner with You, as Head of the Church, in the working of signs, wonders, and miracles in Your name, that the Father in Heaven may be glorified. Please help me in my theology to be more scriptural than traditional, as I have been. May I ever turn to You for direction and headship.

3

RULES: UNDERSTANDING THE HOLY SPIRIT'S PART

Right from the beginning, please note that this is not a chapter on praying to the Holy Spirit. But I am sure we all agree that, while Scripture does not teach us to pray to Him, it certainly does not teach us to *ignore* Him.

How are we to approach this great Third Person of the Trinity? Are we to only be aware that He exists? Are we to know how He functions? Are we to know the perimeters in which He functions? Are we to know what is so unique about Him that differs from the Father and the Son?

I believe the answer to all those questions is, "Yes." This means we should, and must, be approaching Him as a separate Being. We should study to know the rules that differ in going to the Father and the Son, and yet *not* divide the Trinity. Please read the following verses very carefully.

> **And grieve not the holy Spirit of God, whereby ye are sealed unto the day of redemption.**
>
> **Ephesians 4:30**

> **But they rebelled, and vexed his holy Spirit: therefore he was turned to be their enemy, and he fought against them.**
>
> **Isaiah 63:10**

And whosoever shall speak a word against the Son of man, it shall be forgiven him: but unto him that blasphemeth against the Holy Ghost it shall not be forgiven.

Luke 12:10

Quench not the Spirit.

1 Thessalonians 5:19

Wherefore I give you to understand, that no man speaking by the Spirit of God calleth Jesus accursed: and that no man can say that Jesus is the Lord, but by the Holy Ghost.

1 Corinthians 12:3

What awesome position is given to the blessed Holy Spirit! The very pointed and direct warning to refrain from grieving (offending) the Holy Spirit is not to be taken lightly. As most Christians are familiar with the emblem of the Spirit as a dove, this warning takes on even greater meaning. The dove, of all fowls of the air, is most easily offended or grieved.

I recall hearing a story about a small boy who saw a dove on the sill outside his window during a vicious winter storm. He ran to get some bread crumbs to feed it. When he opened the window, the dove flew away, so he left the crumbs on the window ledge. Soon the dove came back and ate them. This went on for some time, and the dove began to trust him to the extent of eating from his hand. One day the boy put out his hand with the bread crumbs and, as was its custom, the meek dove hopped over to eat as usual. As he began to eat, on a mischievous impulse, the boy closed his hand. The dove waited hopefully, and the boy opened his hand. As the dove began to eat, the boy closed his hand again. This happened twice more, then the dove flew away — never to return.

The stern warning by the Apostle Paul, concerning grieving the Holy Spirit, is not to be taken lightly. The Greek word *lupeo* can be translated "grieve, distress, make sorry," and some say "painful." It is a word that, even in English, means "to suffer."

Do we cause the Holy Spirit to suffer?

Do we cause Him pain?

Do we discourage Him?

Do we offend Him?

I am sure the answer is a firm, "Yes," to each of those questions, and we do those things many times without being fully aware of what we are doing. Just as Lot vexed his soul with the ungodly, so we by our carelessness grieve the Third Person of the Trinity. An unholy act, a careless and idle word, a criticism spoken out against another saint, frivolous words — sometimes with double meaning, words that damage relationships, all of these can grieve the Holy Spirit within us and, ultimately, damage the Body of Christ.

Let me say, in language as strong as possible: Be aware of this member of the Trinity in you. He is God's gift to you. Treat Him as the friend that He is and wants to be, the Comforter that He is, the Advocate that He is, the One called alongside to "take-hold-together-against with." He is your Helper.

The breaking of the seal, whereby you are sealed by Him, will allow spiritual light to escape and worldly darkness to creep into your soul so that coldness and lethargy slowly begins to take over. Notice that Israel vexed God's Holy Spirit by its rebellion. The Israelites were turned over to the enemy, and even the Holy Spirit became their enemy.

Many a church member has stirred up trouble against the pastor and church leadership, splitting the church and stopping growth, even putting the pastor out of ministry. Surely this has grieved the Holy Spirit whereby they were sealed and has now caused Him to become their enemy! The very sad truth is that, even as Samson of old, the Holy Spirit has left them, but they are unaware of it and may not realize it until Judgment Day. A little criticism here, a little gossip there, a devious question that will trigger suspicion and doubt.

These are all done so carelessly, yet the aftermath is such that wreaks havoc in the church. A church is stopped in its growth and ministry and little lambs have been wounded. Do not be guilty, as the little boy in the illustration, of drawing back that one more time. Do not tempt Him, but reach out in fellowship and love, and He will respond. All of us need all of the help we can receive from Him in our spiritual relationship with God.

Let me now respond to anyone who might state, "We cannot divide the Trinity." I recognize the unity of the Trinity and understand it to be a great doctrine of the Christian Church through all of the ages. I am not the one raising this question of entreating the members of the Godhead separately. The Scripture clearly teaches that we are to be very knowledgeable concerning the separate office functions of each member of the Trinity.

For example, Jesus taught that the Holy Spirit would not speak of Himself but would speak of Jesus and would remind the disciples of what Jesus had said to them. (John 16:13,14.) The Holy Spirit did this so well that they were able to recall accurately the many things Jesus had taught them. This is why we have the scriptural accounts of the life and teachings of Jesus passed on to us so authentically.

The scriptures also call to our attention that sin against the Holy Spirit is to be treated differently than sin against the other two members of the Trinity. The sin of blasphemy will not be forgiven. Most scholars agree that it is that sin of attributing the works of God to the devil. Perhaps few have committed this sin in our day that we know about. But many were guilty in Jesus' day.

Another great truth emphasized by the scriptures is the teaching in the 12th chapter of 1 Corinthians, instructing us that the control of the nine gifts of the Spirit belong to the Holy Spirit: **But the manifestation of the Spirit is given to every man to profit withal** (1 Cor. 12:7). Then Paul goes on in that chapter to relate how the Holy Spirit gives the administration of one of those gifts to the believer *as He wills,* and that all of these gifts to the Body work by the selfsame Spirit.

If we, as the Church, can truly believe that these gifts are under the control of the Holy Spirit, should not we then proceed to have a better relationship with Him? Should we not be hungry to have healings and miracles among us? Do we wait upon Him for His gifts? Are we fully conscious that He is the One Who distributes them? Are we aware that without Him the gifts do not function? Do we fully understand that we are to covet the best gifts earnestly? Do we fully understand how we grieve Him by our selfishness? Do we fully understand how we offend Him by the wrong use of our tongue? Do we fully understand that it is the Holy Spirit, and Him alone, for which blasphemy is unpardonable? Do we fully understand that there is no conviction of sin, either in a nation or in a church, if the Holy Spirit is withdrawn?

If the preceding facts serve to awaken or alert us as to the importance of the person of the Holy Spirit, then we should face the truth and necessity of the anointing that comes by Him. Our Lord Jesus Christ did not enter into His earthly ministry until the Holy Spirit, as a dove, came upon Him. Following this experience, He then read the scriptures from the Old Testament in the presence of the Jewish leaders.

> **The Spirit of the Lord is upon me, because he hath anointed me to preach the gospel to the poor; he hath sent me to heal the brokenhearted, to preach deliverance to the captives, and recovering of sight to the blind, to set at liberty them that are bruised,**
>
> **To preach the acceptable year of the Lord.**
>
> **Luke 4:18,19**

Under what mighty anointing He ministered! What mighty miracles, signs, and wonders followed Him! The lame were healed, evil spirits cast out, blind people saw, the deaf heard, the multitudes were fed, and the storms obeyed Him! If the anointing He had was totally because of the Holy Spirit, is it not possible for us, also, to have it? Acts 1:8 teaches us that we can.

> **But ye shall receive *power*, after that the Holy Ghost is come upon you: and ye shall be witnesses unto me**

both in Jerusalem, and in all Judea, and in Samaria, and unto the uttermost part of the earth.

The obvious question is, "Why do we not have this power?" A prime answer might be that it lies in our relationship with Him. We must *improve* our relationship. May the following summary be a blessing to you as you search your heart.

Summary

1. Be aware of the work of the Holy Spirit in your life.

2. While we do not suggest that you should pray to Him, *diligent attention* should be given to seeking Him for His help.

3. Seek, constantly, the Third Person of the Trinity — the Spirit of God and His gifts.

4. As you have waited on God, take time to wait on the Holy Spirit for His help and anointing.

5. Freely and honestly confess any neglect of Him.

6. Constantly affirm His rightful place in the Church and in your heart.

7. Repent of, and confess, that which would offend Him.

8. If the unpardonable sin is attributing the works of God to the adversary, the reverse of this is to give more praise and honor to God through the works of the Holy Spirit. Thus, instead of grieving Him, we are pleasing Him.

9. Do not disparage ministries that differ from the one you are involved in or that you have. In so doing, you are running the risk of disparaging the work of the Holy Spirit, thus limiting His freedom to work in your own life.

10. Pray more with the Spirit in your spiritual language (not understood by man), thus entering into His work and partnering with Him.

Prayer

Thank You, Father, for giving me Your precious gift, the Holy Spirit. I ask forgiveness if I have been guilty of neglecting Him. Please help me to wait on Him more, to cooperate with Him more, and to become more sensitive to Him. And to You, precious Holy Spirit, I welcome being filled and filled again to overflowing with Your presence. I welcome You to work Your gifts through me and to anoint me more and more to minister the Word of God. In the precious name of Jesus, Your Son. Amen.

4
RULES: THE PRAYER
OF PSALM 91

Innumerable believers down through the years have claimed Psalm 91 as one of their favorite portions of scripture. But, although it is called a "favorite," few Christians seem to have reaped its great promises and benefits. While we do have a few testimonies of its fulfillment, we have many, many evidences of accidents, sicknesses, plagues, and people who have become a victim of the snare of the fowler (Satan), the terror by night, and the arrow that flieth by day.

Christians, as well as sinners, have succumbed to the pestilence of darkness and the destruction at noonday. Thousands have fallen at the side, and it did devastate Christians, along with sinners, to behold the suffering. Plagues, famines, floods, and earthquakes have taken a terrible toll.

Is there anything in this wonderful psalm that gives us hope, or is it like a good-luck charm that works for some and not others? While many Christians have glorious testimonies, probably more have failed to survive. We are stirred to ask why?

The axiom, different rules for different prayers, applies as much to this psalm as to the other promises dealt with in this book. There is no automatic answer

31

to prayers. Answers to promises and prayers may seem to just happen but, in reality, do not. Certain prayer principles must be believed, acted upon, and the rules must be kept.

The First Group of Promises: Psalm 91:3-8

Let me treat each group of promises in this great psalm in the light of the rule that applies to it.

Surely he shall deliver thee from the snare of the fowler, and from the noisome pestilence.

He shall cover thee with his feathers, and under his wings shalt thou trust: his truth shall be thy shield and buckler.

Thou shalt not be afraid for the terror by night; nor for the arrow that flieth by day;

Nor for the pestilence that walketh in darkness; nor for the destruction that wasteth at noonday.

A thousand shall fall at thy side, and ten thousand at thy right hand; but it shall not come nigh thee.

Only with thine eyes shalt thou behold and see the reward of the wicked.

Psalm 91:3-8

These promises deal with deliverance from Satan (the fowler), epidemics, fear, and plagues. While multitudes have quoted, claimed, and hoped, few have received the benefits of these specific promises. Many people overlook the fact that these promises are prefaced with a mandatory rule: **He that dwelleth in the secret place of the most High shall abide under the shadow of the Almighty** (Ps.91:1).

While there are millions of Christians who name the name of Jesus, there are few who live and abide in the shadow of the deity of our God, the great and awesome Trinity. The word *dwelleth*, meaning "to live," is a good Hebrew word with varied meanings. It is the word *yashab*, and it literally means to "sit in the seat." It is more of a fixed position than coming, going, or moving about. It is not the picture of a wavering saint, one who blows hot and cold, in victory one day and out the next, nor is it a picture of one who is consistently lukewarm. Certainly, it is not a picture of one who frequently backslides!

This word paints a picture of one who makes up his mind to serve God, love God, and be in a fixed position as regards his relationship with God. This man will repose under His great shadow and protection. It is God's responsibility to protect that saint who lives, abides, and dwells in His great covering, shielding, protecting shadow. Satan cannot seize you or harm you in that place of sanctuary with God.

Note very carefully the second rule for this first section of promises: **I will say of the Lord** (Ps. 91:2). This may be the most overlooked verse in the entire psalm. Not only are many Christians careless with their speech, but many have mocked those who do believe it is important to speak positively concerning the events of their lives, to *bridle* their tongues, as it is stated in James 3.

Please note again, however, what people say who abide under the shadow of the Almighty: **I will *say* of the Lord.** These people are living and abiding under the shadow of the Almighty and, because they are, they sound like it. They talk like it. Their conversation sounds as the conversation of a citizen of Heaven ought to sound. Christians endeavoring to live under God's great shadow cannot talk as they once talked when they were in the world.

Isaiah 8:20 helps us to understand how much importance God places upon our speech: **To the law and to the testimony: if they *speak* not according to this word, it is because there is no *light* in them.** A possible paraphrase of this verse might read like this: "There is a heavenly law and a testimony that will reveal to all whether you have light (glory) or not, and you will let this be known by your words." God's children should not only *act* like His children, they should *sound* like His children.

Ephesians 4:22 admonishes us to put off the former conversation. Verse 25 tells us that we are to put away lying and speak truth. Verse 29 says to let *no* corrupt conversation or words come out of our mouths, only that which is good and will edify the hearers. I realize that the *King James* translation is about the only one that uses *conversation* in this sense. But, after many years of study — including how it is used in the Greek — I agree with them! After all, your speech, more than your lifestyle, will locate your spiritual relationship. Your speech always will betray and identify you.

This great rule best can be summarized by Psalm 19:14: **Let the words of my mouth, and the meditation of my heart, be acceptable in thy sight, O Lord, my strength, and my redeemer.** You cannot claim sickness and accidents with your mouth and still believe in your heart that God has you under His feathers with His truth being your shield and buckler. Don't let the vast coverage of human tragedies and national disasters by the news media bring fear into your heart. It will eventually become a part of your daily conversation.

Notice all the benefits that are available because you *dwell in the secret place of the Most High*, daily confessing that God is your refuge and fortress and that you trust in Him: deliverance from the snare of the fowler and pestilence (epidemics), being covered by God's feathers (presence), having His truth as a shield and buckler, free from terror by night and arrows by day, safe from destruction, and protection, although a thousand or ten thousand fall at your side.

These great and grand results are only for those who keep and obey the rules. It is not automatic just because you are a Christian. If that were so, no Christian would ever get sick or be involved in an accident.

The Second Group of Promises — Psalm 91:10-13

Notice what precedes the next group of promises: **Because thou hast made the Lord, which is my refuge, even the most High, thy habitation** (Ps. 91:9). This is the rule that brings the promises to fruition.

> **There shall no evil befall thee, neither shall any plague come nigh thy dwelling.**
>
> **For he shall give his angels charge over thee, to keep thee in all thy ways.**
>
> **They shall bear thee up in their hands, lest thou dash thy foot against a stone.**
>
> **Thou shalt tread upon the lion and adder: the young lion and the dragon shalt thou trample under feet.**
>
> **Psalm 91:10-13**

This group of promises says we can be free from evil and free from plagues, that we can have angelic protection to the point of not even stumbling, and that we can have the power to tread all over the power of the enemy. As Deuteronomy 28:13 promises:

> **The Lord shall make thee the head, and not the tail; and thou shalt be above only, and thou shalt not be beneath; if that thou hearken to the commandments of the Lord thy God.**

The above precious promises, claimed by so many of God's people down through the years, can only be fulfilled for you if, by your will and determination, you have become by "habit" a lover and seeker of the throne of God. His presence at the throne must be your preferential choice. You must want to be with Him more than with anyone else you know or love.

I heard of a man of God who did not have a good marriage, and who met a Christian woman whose life concepts were much like his own. Although there was a spark of interest, he would not allow even his thoughts to proceed any further. To do so would have been sin that would have separated him from the Lord. God had become his refuge and his habitation, his first love, and he wouldn't do anything to jeopardize that relationship.

The Third Group of Promises — Psalm 91:15,16

The rule for receiving the last set of benefits is closely related to that for the second group: **Because he hath set his love upon me** (Ps. 91:14). The second rule dealt with the soul, the hunger to constantly be in His presence. This one deals more with the spirit, the heart of man. Setting one's love upon God is spiritual worship at its greatest. Jesus said love was the greatest commandment, and rightly so. To love God with all of one's heart is far above all else and meets all of His requirements.

God can overlook many of the weaknesses which we all have when He knows of our great love for Him. King David should have been stoned to death because of his crime of passion that resulted in the murder of an innocent man. But God allowed him to live because, from his days as a shepherd boy, he had loved God with all of his heart. When he was brought by the prophet Nathan to a realization of what he had done, he repented sorely.

Friend, if your attempts at all else fail, keep loving God. Notice these last benefits are yours as you keep this rule of love: complete deliverance, lifted high above all danger with full and continued protection, continual answers to prayer, honor on your life that only God can give, and a good, long life, free of trouble.

Many pages have been written on this, one of the greatest of all the psalms. It does not seem necessary to repeat in detail all of the height and depth of meaning in these verses. I merely call the attention of the reader to the rules that must be obeyed. While no promise of God is void of power, these promises do not automatically operate in the lives of Christians, who are not immune to the accidents of life. There seem to be a few in every Christian community, however, who relate such rich, glowing testimonies of God's saving and keeping power. Some even tell of seeing their angels during times when they needed protection.

Psalm 91 is rich and rewarding, but the rules must be kept for it to be effective. Please learn them and make them your own. Practice them until they become a habit. Seek to *abide, obey,* and, above all else, *love Him* with all your heart.

Prayer

Father, please forgive me for not abiding under Your great shadow as I should. Forgive me for careless speech that expressed fear rather than faith. Help me to show my love to You in daily worship, for I want more than anything else in this life to live a long life with all of Your benefits. In the name of the Lord Jesus. Amen.

5

RULES: THE PRAYER
OF PSALM 37:4

This chapter deals with receiving your heart's desires, not through prayer, but through another principle.

Delight thyself also in the Lord; and he shall give thee the desires of thine heart.

Psalm 37:4

Other ways to say this might be "seek your pleasure in the Lord" or "make the Lord your only joy." The Hebrew word translated "delight" is *A-nag (aw-nag)*. It means to be "soft and pliable" as a maiden who finds the one man she desires and makes him her one and only love. It is as you make God your Lord, and Jesus your only true friend above all family and friendships — although you love them dearly — that you will receive the desires of your heart.

Going to church and gathering with the saints is never a chore to be suffered, an unpleasant duty to be performed unwillingly, *if* you want to receive the desires of your heart. Instead, gathering with other saints who are like-minded, going into the presence of the Lord with much praise and much thanksgiving, always looking forward to that glorious day when we will all be together with Him forever, is true and pure delight — if you do so willingly and joyfully.

Paying our tithes and giving our offerings to the Lord with great joy must delight Him. In some churches, the congregations break into praise and joy when the tithes and offerings are received. They give, not grudgingly or of necessity, but willingly and joyfully.

Those who perform the many necessary duties of the church with joy are delighting themselves in the Lord. Unsung responsibilities such as taking care of youngsters while others enjoy the services, working long hours to keep the house of worship beautiful and in repair, preparing and helping serve during the happy times of fellowship in the church, and visiting homes, hospitals, and prisons can all be a part of delighting in the Lord.

A good example in the Old Testament is the time when Judah served the Lord under King Asa.

> They entered into a covenant to seek the Lord God of their fathers with all of their heart and with all their soul;
>
> That whosoever would not seek the Lord God of Israel should be put to death, whether small or great, whether man or woman.
>
> And they sware unto the Lord with a loud voice, and with shouting, and with trumpets, and with coronets.
>
> And all Judah rejoiced at the oath: for they had sworn with all their heart, and sought him with their whole desire; and he was found of them: and the Lord gave them rest round about.
>
> **2 Chronicles 15:12-15**

Seldom, indeed, do we find a people who will do what we have just read. Israel and Judah seemingly were always in trouble with wars, famines, pestilence, and slavery. During the times they greatly rejoiced in serving the Lord God of Israel, they had rest — their greatest desire. God warned Israel against half-hearted service. In Deuteronomy 28, we find the blessings of God that were promised when they served Him. Also, we find the curses that were to come upon them if they turned from serving Him.

The blessings included complete health and prosperity. Whether in the city or the field, whatever they put their hand to was to be blessed. They were to be "the head, not the tail" and were to be so prospered that they would never have to borrow but would have plenty to lend.

If they turned from serving the Lord, then the curse would fall upon them. All of the above blessings would leave and, instead, they would experience sickness instead of health, poverty instead of plenty, their children would be put out to slavery, another would eat the crops they had planted, and they would be smitten with everything that constantly plagued the heathen. Instead of being overtaken by blessings, the curse would come.

We have read of the great failure in their history, continuing even to this century in the holocaust of World War II when millions of Jews were cruelly tortured and slain. Why? What would cause a people to have and to enjoy so much and then allow it to be taken from them? To have had the greatest, the epitome of everything, and then, suddenly, be without anything!

Let us be honest. We, who have covenanted with the Son of God and who are the Church that claims the name of Jesus, have organized and meet together to sing from the hymn book and read from the Bible. We study the Word and build church buildings. But how do most Christians fare? Are they exempt from having to borrow? Are they free from sickness, accidents, divorce, financial bondage? Are most of the churches free from splits and quarrels and gossip? These are some of the "curses" that seem to abound.

If the answers to the above questions seem to be more "no" than "yes," then the average church and the average Christian are as much under the curse (or more so) as under the blessings.

Is there an answer to this dilemma? I believe that there is — the same answer that would have solved the problems of the Israelites when they failed to receive their desire from the Lord. The answer is found in Deuteronomy 28:47,48.

> **Because thou servedst not the Lord thy God with joyfulness, and with gladness of heart, for the abundance of all things;**
>
> **Therefore shalt thou serve thine *enemies* which the Lord shall send against thee, in hunger, and in thirst, and in nakedness, and in want of all things.**

The Hebrew word *abad* translated here as "servedst" is sometimes translated "worship." To paraphrase the rule for this chapter, "Have fun in the Lord," with even the thought implied of sport. Enjoy whatever you do that is connected with serving or worshipping God.

Do we observe this? Do we see people gathering together in joyfulness, almost a gala atmosphere, laughing and rejoicing before the Lord? Do we hear and see joyfulness expressed when the offering is mentioned? Do Christians accept with joy the responsibilities that might be considered mundane, happy that these duties represent something they can do, as it were, for Jesus? Do we really want the desires of our heart, even peace and tranquility and rest from the enemy?

If so, here are some summary guidelines and rules for receiving the promise of Psalm 37:4.

Summary Rules

1. Do all that you can for Jesus, Head of the Church, with great joy.

2. Seek ways to serve Him and do them with joy, especially if these are tasks that someone else has turned down.

3. Be careful when you tithe that you cause yourself to rejoice. (Note to pastors: Encourage your congregation to be audible in their joy at the privilege of giving to the Lord.) If you feel a little pain at parting with your money, give a little more! It is the same as saying to the devil, "If you don't leave me alone, I will double my tithe."

4. Be very careful not to put down another brother or sister. It is the same as putting down the Lord Jesus, inasmuch as we are one in Him.

43

5. Look forward with joy to your times with the Lord, to fasting, prayer, Bible study and reading, to gathering with the saints.

Do the above and receive the desires, the longings of your heart — those things which are, of course, in His will. Become the head and not the tail. Be able to lend instead of borrowing. Be blessed in the city and in the field. Be blessed coming in and going out. Be able to put to flight your enemies and have them flee seven ways to get away from you. Be blessed with a good spouse, children, and grandchildren. Be greatly blessed in whatever you put your hand to, in your work time and leisure time.

It seems to me that the first step to backsliding or growing lukewarm is the *loss of joy*. The next step, just before slipping back into deep sin, could be losing your *spirit of thanksgiving*. Romans 1:21 says: **Because that, when they knew God, they glorified him not as God, neither were thankful; but became vain in their imagination, and their foolish heart was darkened.**

I have never seen a Christian backslide who always was full of joy and thankfulness. These two beautiful qualities seem to go together. Many times people, who once had an experience with the Lord, go back into hard, deep sin because they cease to give thanks to God for their salvation, for the Bible, for the privilege of living in this great nation, for the freedom to worship. When they ceased in this, their foolish hearts became darkened. Even when you do not feel bubbling, effervescent joy, don't fail to give grateful thanks to God for loving you and for sending Jesus. Psalm 37:4 should now yield beautiful lasting beneficial heart desires. Apply the rules and reap the benefits!

Prayer

Father, in Jesus' name, it will make me very happy to have the desires of my heart, and I will guard against covetousness and selfishness. Please correct me when serving You begins to become a chore instead of a joy. May I, with Your help, begin each day with thankfulness, joy, and anticipation for what the day will bring forth. I promise You that I will serve You, worship You, give of myself and my substance to You with great delight. Please forgive me for those times when I failed in these things, and help me to be more aware of serving You with joy and delighting to do Your will. Help me to be more like Your Son, Who, for the joy that was set before Him, endured His cross. Help me, my Father, in Jesus' name, to never, never become weary in well doing. Amen.

6
RULES: MOVING A MOUNTAIN

The rules for moving a mountain ought to be of great interest to everyone, especially to Christians. Even worldly minded people kick against barriers or hindrances in the way of their progress. It really doesn't matter whether it is a family, financial, or physical barrier, all of us want it out of the way. To the people of Judah in Jesus' day, a mountain represented any hindrance to their progress. So when Jesus told them they could have whatever they said, even to the moving of a mountain, they could easily identify with what he was teaching. How many of them believed what He taught is a different matter. How many of us believe, literally, Mark 11:23 and 24 today?

And on the morrow, when they were come from Bethany, he was hungry:

And seeing a fig tree afar off having leaves, he came, if haply he might find any thing thereon: and when he came to it, he found nothing but leaves; for the time of figs was not yet.

And Jesus answered and said unto it, No man eat fruit of thee hereafter for ever. And his disciples heard it.

Mark 11:12-14

And when even was come, he went out of the city.

And in the morning, as they passed by, they saw the fig tree dried up from the roots.

And Peter calling to remembrance saith unto him, Master, behold, the fig tree which thou cursedst is withered away.

47

And Jesus answering saith unto them, Have faith in God.

For verily I say unto you, That whosoever shall say unto this mountain, Be thou removed, and be thou cast into the sea; and shall not doubt in his heart, but shall believe that those things which he saith shall come to pass; he shall have whatsoever he saith.

Therefore I say unto you, What things soever ye desire, when ye pray, believe that ye receive them, and ye shall have them.

Mark 11:19-24

The rules for moving a mountain cannot be understood until there is some understanding of what particular hindrance you are wishing to move, an understanding not only of the hindrance itself but of how it came to be there in your way. Let me explain.

If you have produced a financial mountain by lack of wisdom in handling finances, you will not be free to move it. If your mountain is a physical illness, and you are aware that you are not eating properly or taking care of your physical body, no effort to move that mountain will be successful until you correct the problem that allowed it to grow.

The First Rule for Moving a Mountain

The first rule, then, would be not to build the mountain in the first place!

The Lord spoke to me and said, *Teach my people that I will not allow them to become mountain movers as long as they are building them.*

In other words, praying to move mountains will not work if, at the same time, we are responsible for

Rules: Moving a Mountain

them being there and not prepared to do anything about the actions that built them. If an illness is caused by deep-seated resentment, that must be taken care of before an attempt is made to move the mountain.

I heard about an elderly man and his wife who suddenly were in much need of medical attention. Finally, their doctor asked when the symptoms began. They answered that the problems began about the time they began to have trouble with a neighbor. The physician, a wise man, asked them if they didn't think it might be a good idea to take care of the trouble with the neighbor first. When they did, their symptoms left!

Now, let's talk about the second rule for moving a mountain. In these verses, Jesus was not talking about prayer. He didn't ask God the Father to move the mountain. Prayer to God, asking Him to move a mountain in the above context is *praying beyond the limit God has set with man.* He would be violating His own principle of not interfering with our free wills, and violating His own laws is beyond His ability to do.

The Second Rule for Moving a Mountain

In Mark 11:22, Jesus refers to the faith of God or the God-kind of faith, but no mention is made of prayer. Jesus did not teach us to believe and expect God to move the mountain. The teaching is that we are to believe and expect the mountain to move *because we believe.* We move the mountain because we believe, in expectancy, that the hindrance will go. Doesn't it make sense to you that, if we can create one, we should be able to move it?

With this rule comes clear understanding that we must act as His children in authority. Without understanding, we cannot act with that authority. There will be other prayers addressed to Him for specific things, but not for moving a mountain. Be certain to read all the rules for all the different types of prayer.

Our words carry much more authority than we realize. If we really did believe we could have mountain-moving words flowing out of our lips, I am sure we would be more careful about the words we speak — especially of the words that contribute to the building of mountains.

When the disciples saw what happened to the fig tree, they must have desired to have like faith. The first thing Jesus taught them was that they could do as He did by speaking to the mountain. By talking directly to the mountain or the hindrance, whatever it was, it could be moved.

The first time the word "say" is used in the 23rd verse, it comes from the Greek word, *lego*. The second time it is used, it is the Greek word, *epo*, which is used in Mark 1:44 where Jesus commands the man to say (*epo*) nothing to any man. It is a strong verb with a strong past tense meaning "you have said" or "you have been saying." In other words, it means speaking with a command in your voice, being firm. (See Strong's concordance for further thoughts.[1])

To confirm how strong this command to the mountain becomes, notice how firm and powerful the Greek makes it: "And throw yourself into the sea." So *the second great rule is commanding, or knowing, that what you are saying is correct.*

50

You are not only saying it now, but this has been your confession for some time, and you plan to continue saying it. Thus, faith and correct speaking become a lifestyle rather than a formula or a way out of your trouble.

The Third Rule for Moving a Mountain

This brings us to the third rule: *bringing your heart into alignment with your tongue.* You are now, and you have been, saying strong words (*epo*). You plan to keep on saying them, and you will make your heart line up with your mouth. Jesus said, **and shall not doubt in his heart.** That is a very important statement. In the New Testament era, they wrote about a "cultural sickness of confidence" or a sense of much doubt. Wavering or doubting is suggested by W. E. Vine as, "Not so much a weakness of faith, as a lack of it . . . implying uncertainty."[2]

In Mark 11:23 and Matthew 21:21, man has the promise of God, and he clings to it when he speaks the Word of faith to God or to the mountain. But if he still thinks it impossible or is not certain that what he says should be done, he is at odds with himself. He believes, and yet he does not believe. Doubt is, from the outset, a breach of a great principle. It is a breach which excludes God's help.

We must have the ability to overcome our unbelief, or Jesus would never have asked us to eschew it. The Word of God also warned Israel of unbelief and reminded them of its frightful price. Everyone who seeks to pray must deal with unbelief. Notice that Jesus told us where doubt is located — in the heart.

Those who study the brain are convinced that it is divided into layers. Some say there are two sides to the brain, the right and the left. When people have strokes, it depends on where the blood from the ruptured blood vessel damages the brain as to where the body is affected. There seems to be a part of the brain, however, that is never affected. People who became comatose will relate later that they were aware of what was going on around them.

When Jesus mentioned doubt being in the heart, we know He was not speaking about the physical organ but a part of us with which we can believe and can experience affectionate love and emotions.

We have power over this part of our brain, to improve it. We can deal with unbelief, doubt, and fear. Thus we can change. Some years ago, I took flying lessons in a small plane. I had to deal with much fear. As knowledge of how the airplane functioned became familiar, much of the fear began to leave. So it is in everything that knowledge is the greatest method of dealing with unbelief and doubt. Fear results from a lack of knowledge.

Feed your mind continually with great positive truths from God's Word, and you will discover doubt will begin to leave. A simple illustration comes from the medical profession. They tell us that many people are brought into the emergency room with heavy chest pain, believing they are having a heart attack. After tests, they are informed that nothing is wrong with their heart. They were suffering from gas pains. Immediately upon finding out they do not have a serious problem, all fear will leave.

A good suggestion is to memorize certain scriptures that deal with things that can become a mountain to you.

The Fourth Rule for Moving a Mountain

The last rule for moving that mountain is *believing you will have whatever you say*. It is difficult to name any one of the rules as most important, but this last rule must have priority. You could do all of the other rules set forth in this chapter, but if you miss this last one — *believing you will have whatever you say*, you will not be able to move your mountain.

You must believe your words are powerful. You must believe that you will have whatever you say. Jesus is the one who said it, not some aspiring "faith teacher." Believe this, not only in the positive aspect, but in the negative. You will reap the seed sown by your tongue.

Be afraid to talk negative. Be afraid to claim sickness with your tongue. Believe so strongly in the principle that Jesus taught that you will watch what you say. You just might reap it!

No chapter on rules for moving the mountain will be complete without using illustrations. The best one ever recorded is the one concerning the rebuilding of the city and temple in Jerusalem under the leadership of Zerubbabel after the remnant of the Jews returned from exile in Babylon.

For who are you, O great mountain [of human obstacles]? Before Zerubbabel [who with Joshua had led the return of the exiles from Babylon and was undertaking the rebuilding of the temple, before him] you shall become a plain [a mere mole hill]! And he

shall bring forth the finishing gable stone [of the new temple] with loud shoutings of the people, crying, Grace, grace to it!

Zechariah 4:7 AMP

This great example supplies a fitting climax to the chapter that gives the rules for moving a mountain. How the Church has missed such a great teaching and example such as this is difficult to understand.

There was a great mountain, and it was removed by speaking directly to it. The Word tells us what to say. By shouting or crying, *"Grace,"* to the mountain, it was removed to a mere mole hill and was no longer a hindrance. This is what God intends. By obeying His Word, we speak directly to hindrances, which will be reduced and done away with because we believe in God's Word and carry out even the slightest of His commands.

I have had some personal experiences, and have had many others related to me, that demonstrate the power of speaking "grace" to the hindrance. "Grace" is a great Bible word that means more than just the unmerited favor of God. We are eternally grateful for that meaning, of course, but the word also implies the power of God. (Acts 4:33.) God's power moves by grace and not by our own worth. Many are the victories of God's saints who act in faith, believing. Be one of them. Move your mountain. Speak to it in faith, believing your own words!

To summarize these rules, please note that we are not referring to prayer. This problem which we are addressing has grown to such a proportion that prayer will not work. You now have a mountain. There are, at times — financial burdens, sicknesses, marital problems — that get so big they hinder all progress. They have become a mountain that must be moved. You have gone the route of prayer to no avail, so no need to continue that direction. You *must* move that mountain!

Now that you have read this chapter, you realize that Jesus made you to be a mountain mover. Speak to that mountain with authority, calling it by name. Say, "You mountain of (name sickness, debt, etc.), I command you to move! Throw yourself into the sea. Be gone, as I shout grace, grace, to you!" Now that you have taken this bold step, do not doubt your words. Believe the scriptures. Keep speaking "grace" to that mountain, and firmly believe that you will have what you say. You are now a mountain mover!

Prayer

Dear Father, I believe I am who You say I am and that I will become all that You say I can become. Through Your help, I will stop building mountains and will become a mountain mover. I will watch the words of my mouth that they do not contradict my heart. I will speak "grace" to the mountain that is before me that hinders my physical and spiritual progress. It will have to move and give way to the power of God that flows from my mouth. In Jesus' name. Amen.

---

[1] James Strong, *Strong's Exhaustive Concordance of the Bible* (Nashville: Abingdon Press, 1890).

[2] W. E. Vine, *An Expository Dictionary of New Testament Words* (Old Tappan: Fleming H. Revell Co., 1966).

7
RULES: MARK 11:24

Notice how clear and plain the mark of distinction is between Mark 11:23 and Mark 11:24 because of the word "therefore." The word "therefore" is a very, very strong adverb, even a strong adversity word. It is a word that very definitely makes one to know something is being contrasted. Not only is there a great contrast between verses 23 and 24 but also a strong emphasis on what is said in verse 24.

Where many students miss the full impact is in not noticing that Jesus is not merely continuing a thought but is contrasting the two verses. His use of therefore infers, "I have told you the former thing so that I can lead you into this latter thing. I have told you how to move a mountain, a hindrance, a barrier, now I tell you how to pray to receive the desire of your heart."

Many casual Bible students have concluded that Jesus' whole subject matter was only prayer and not moving a mountain. They do not believe that a child of God has this much authority.

It can be said that anytime you see the word "therefore" it simply means, "Because of the former, I can give you what is to follow." Jesus literally is saying, "Do, practice, put into operation verse 23, and you can then have verse 24." The implication, of course, is that you cannot have verse 24 without first doing verse 23.

Why would Jesus deny us our heart's desire if we did not move a mountain?

Remember the cardinal rule for moving a mountain? Your heart and your mouth must be in perfect agreement. You will not be able to receive the desire of your heart if you fail to keep your tongue and heart saying and believing the same things. Perhaps the greatest illustration we have is Father Abraham who was told by God to offer his only son Isaac on the altar as a burnt sacrifice.

Abraham always had obeyed God's orders. I see him taking his son and some servants into the mountains. He turns to the young men with him and tells them to wait while he and Isaac go up the mountain to worship. He said, **I and the lad will go yonder and worship, and come again to you** (Gen. 22:5). What a confession of faith! God had said to offer Isaac as a burnt sacrifice to Him. Abraham had no scriptural right to go against God's word. Yet Abraham confessed to the servants that both he and Isaac would return! In other words, he said, "I am believing and confessing *beyond* what God told me!"

It disheartens me to hear pastors criticize the faith message, to hear them putting down confession of what God has said in His Word as something to be avoided. Many, I am convinced, do this because they attempt to correct what they consider to be excesses. Abraham is the father of us all. He is the father of the faith. He is the father of faith's confession, even going beyond that of any faith teachers I have ever known, including myself.

His mouth said, speaking out in words that were heard by the servants, "I and my son will return." Why did he say this when God had plainly said, "You will offer him to me." Abraham not only plainly understood the command, but took the fire and the wood and lifted up the knife to slay Isaac. Why then did he confess that he and Isaac would return? He believed in his heart that God would raise Isaac from the dead. (Heb. 11:19.) That is a strong faith! For after he had slain Isaac with a knife, he was to burn him upon the altar!

When can I, or you, make such a confession? Only when we have that kind of a *relationship* with the Father. Dr. Kenneth Hagin relates how that, when he knew that his wife, Oretha, would die, he went to the Lord and said, "She is going to die, isn't she?" The Lord answered, "Yes." Then Dr. Hagin said, "Will you spare her for my sake?" The Lord answered in the affirmative, and she was raised up.

Is this going beyond God's Word? No. Not when you know your God. When you know how He thinks, know His nature, know His great love for you. Faith is given to us, not just to appropriate, but to build that *kind of relationship*. Many Christians, I think, presume upon a relationship that they do not have with God. They do confess the Word, but lack commitment, relationship, and obedience to that same Word.

We cannot ever go beyond what God's Word states specifically. We cannot go beyond a known command. The centurion's faith came very close to Abraham's experience. Jesus said to him, "I will come and heal your servant." (Luke 7.) The centurion knew enough about Jesus and about authority that he said it was not necessary for Jesus to come in person — all He had to do was to speak the word only. Jesus marvelled at his faith and boldness and *therefore* did not have to do what He said He would do.

Now, because you have kept your mouth and heart in harmony, because you have taken care of your mountain, you are now ready for God to give you the *desire* of your heart. The word "desire," even in English, can be either an intensive term or a passive one. It can even be used as a contrast. You might say, "What kind of food do you desire?" The Greek word for desire, *aiteo*, means "to ask, beg, call for, crave, desire, require." Another word is *putho*. It is strictly a demand of something due. (See Strong's concordance.)

Its usage in scripture is not a picture of one having a quick, sudden, desire for something and deciding to use Mark 11:24 to get it. It is more of a deep craving, a longing, almost a requirement, like saying, "I must have this, or I will die."

Do you remember the incident related in Matthew 20 where the mother of James and John requested that her sons be allowed to be seated one on each side of Jesus in His Kingdom? This was not a sudden idea. No doubt James and John had talked about this with their mother for some time. You can, with a little imagination, see her strongly urge Jesus, almost demanding.

Again, in Mark 15:8, the multitude cried aloud desiring (*aiteo*) Pilate to release a prisoner. This request of theirs, or desire, was based on that which usually was done. It was a custom but, again, strong demand is in their voices.

Getting our heart's desire granted to us has a very strong connotation of being something you desire that is in the realm of possibility, as opposed to the impossible. It is almost a life-and-death situation, not the flighty "I would like a new dress or even a car." It is not something based on a fancy.

Getting down to the specific rules for Mark 11:24 will, I trust, make it very clear for the reader to thoroughly understand these rules and apply them.

Principles for Mark 11:24

1. You have been able to establish such a relationship with God that you are already a *mountain mover*.

2. You are not a negative person, not a mountain builder who is a worrier and fearful.

3. You are a person of prayer. It will not be "shocking" to God when you now seek for the desire of your heart.

4. As you pray, you are very definite and specific in your request, and you have already determined it is within the realm of God's will for you.

5. As you pray, you receive a confirmation in your spirit that this desire can be yours.

6. You now believe with all of your heart that it is yours.

7. And the very moment you believe, you know that it is yours forever.

8. You believe so fervently that you now have it in your possession, and you can rejoice over it so much, that when it appears materially you won't need to rejoice over it. You already have done so!

9. Let your words and actions show your belief. Do not pray about it again because that would show a lack of faith in your first prayer.

10. Let your conversation and actions show that you believe it is done.

Prayer

Father, I know that You love me so much and care very deeply for me. You spared nothing in Heaven to give me all I will ever need. I have this deep, deep desire. I know it is in Your Word for me, thus in Your will for me. I believe, even now as I pray, that this desire is mine. I have it. It comes from you, and I rejoice very much that You care that much and did this for me. I rejoice over it and give You thanks for it, for it is mine because You are my Father, and I am Your child. In the name of Jesus, Your Son. Amen.

8
RULES: MATTHEW 18:19

As far as Christians desiring to have something done for them by God, their Father, Matthew 18:19 probably is the greatest verse in the Bible on which to stand. It is so explicit and direct.

Again I say unto you, That if two of you shall agree on earth as touching any thing that they shall ask, it shall be done for them of my Father which is in heaven.

This promise actually teaches that if you can get someone to agree with you, you can receive anything that you ask. Someone may hurriedly object to that statement, saying "It can't be that easy!" And they would be right. There is a catch, and it's not easy. Why is it so difficult to get someone to agree with you? You will notice that Jesus begins this promise with the word *if*. It is a very big if. This word actually introduces a supposition, raising the very large question of "if" it is possible to find two people to agree. This small two-letter word is used hundreds of times in the scriptures. In every case, something hinges on the outcome.

You will remember that God told Abraham what He would do to the sinful city of Sodom. Abraham entreated God "if" He would spare the city "if" he could find 10 righteous people — which he couldn't. God had to proceed with His judgment because a little two-letter word became a giant word. A city was destroyed because of the outcome of "if."

God taught Israel that if she would obey Him, keep His commandments, etc. that He would bless the nation, prosper it, and keep the people in health. Again, the little word "if" became the means of literal death of a nation scattered abroad throughout the world, without a home for centuries.

Another big "if" is found in Mark 9:23. *If thou canst believe.* Over and over again, we see the effects of this life-changing word. Concerning our daily lives, the heartache and tragedies that could have been avoided "if only." If only I had looked both ways. If only I had not left the iron on. If only I had not driven while drunk. If only I had not married so young. If only I had finished college. Time and space will not begin to permit me to write here all of the instances that come to mind concerning this thought.

If you have been caught with this small two-letter word becoming the giant killer that ruined you, you can turn to the Lord Jesus as the only One Who can completely restore and help you.

The Greek word for *agree* means "to symphonize or harmonize." It literally means "sounding together." Adam Clarke writes of it as "playing the same tune." The likelihood of two people, diverse in nature, agreeing so harmoniously together is a possibility, but often not a strong probability.

Finding Someone to Agree

Finding a person to agree with you, who does not have a similar need, is difficult. The reason for this is that the natural and normal thing for a person to do is immediately think of his own similar need when he is approached about agreeing for someone else's need that is similar to his.

For instance, urgency is always to be contended with. If you have a financial need, and you approach a friend to agree with you, perhaps he, or she, has a financial need that also is urgent and it would be difficult to agree single-mindedly with you. It is even possible that when you approach another Christian, asking agreement with you for your burden, that his or her first impulse will be to think, "What do I need?" or "My need is greater than yours."

If you are unmarried and praying about a mate for life, it would be better to go to someone already happily married who can give undivided attention to agreeing with you. If you're in need of finances, don't go to someone who also needs money. It is not that we are so selfish, but just very human. I have never heard of receiving a request based on agreement by finding someone and saying, "If you will agree with me, I will agree with you." That would be hitting some musical note together and holding it. That's like saying, "I will try to hit your note, if you will hit mine."

One great truth to remember when you are endeavoring to stand on the Word of God is to be as technical as you possibly can. Notice this verse we are dealing with doesn't say anything about a prayer, either a short one or a long one. All it suggests is that nothing more needs to happen other than just two people agreeing.

Some time ago, while I was serving as an overseer of churches, I was being flown throughout the northwest area of the United States by a Christian brother using his own aircraft. He often said to me that we needed a more fully equipped airplane that would handle the freezing weather in the altitudes in which we were flying. His plane also lacked the turbo-charged engines that the mountainous areas required.

One night, after hearing me teach on prayer and faith, he said to me, "When are you going to ask God for that better airplane we need?" At that very moment, this great verse of scripture came out of my spirit, **If two of you shall agree . . .** And I said, "Because you know the requirements better than I do, you state exactly what we need. I will *agree* with you, and we will have it."

He named the specifications as being "a late model, six-passenger, twin-engine, turbo-charge, fully equipped for de-icing, and fully radioed." I said, "I agree. We will get our plane, as you have just described."

Of course, I said this by faith. Everything we get from God, we get by faith. Every time I passed an airport and saw a plane such as I just described, I would say, "Ours is coming!" A few months later, a local businessman invited me out to breakfast and, just before we were ready to leave, handed me a set of keys to a six-passenger Seneca II with all of the equipment we requested! Following are some rules exemplified in this incident that are applicable to all who desire to stand on Matthew 18:19.

10 Rules for Standing on Matthew 18:19

1. This desire of my heart was not a selfish one. It was for ministry.

2. This request was based specifically on Matthew 18:19.

3. Both of us fully agreed, single-mindedly, on every detail.

4. We did not repeat the request. To have done so would have broken the agreement.

5. After agreeing, we gave thanks as though we already had the plane.

6. We never broke agreement by talking in a negative or doubtful way.

7. The free use of a $100,000 airplane did not cause us to be puffed up with pride. Instead, it humbled us inasmuch as it was His gift to us.

8. This testimony is a great encouragement to all who hear it.

9. The timing was correct. It was not done impulsively and without consideration.

10. The answer to Matthew 18:19 not only blessed us materially and physically but also spiritually.

Additional Guidelines

1. Do not use Matthew 18:19 to fill a desire of your heart that could be out of greed or selfishness.

2. Don't be rushed into asking someone to agree with you. Be patient and pray much about timing.

3. Be very careful about your choice of persons to agree with you. Don't just pick the first person you see.

4. Take all the time you need in order to ask specifically. Once a lovely young single girl asked me to agree with her for a husband. I questioned her about what characteristics she would like to have in this man, such as: how old, how tall, what color of hair and eyes, vocation, nationality. She had to tell me she didn't know and hadn't thought of all these things. I had her take time to think of answers to all of these questions and then come back to me. Later, she came back with all of these things clearly thought through. We agreed, and a short time later, she was married to a young man who fit all of the things for which she had asked.

5. Don't make the mistake of allowing *presumption* to hinder this agreement. A very ordinary person would be presumptive to ask for a beauty queen to be his bride, or someone on a limited income to ask for a $50,000 luxury car. What we ask someone to agree with us about should be commensurate with our lifestyle and niche in life.

6. Be very careful that you don't ask for something that would make you puffed up or prideful.

Prayer

Dear Heavenly Father, thank You for giving to Your children the power of agreement. You have promised to stand behind that agreement and give us the things we request. I now acknowledge all of my ways to You, and ask You to help me to understand how very much You love me and want me, Your child, to be happy. Please lead me to that person who will agree with me. I only desire those things that are in Your perfect will for my life. In the name of Jesus, Your Son. Amen.

9
RULES: COMMUNION

The very act of receiving and partaking of the sacred sacrament of communion carries with it a wonderful promise of health and happiness and longevity and the great hope of our Lord's coming. Yet countless Christians, partaking of the Lord's Supper as they regularly attend their churches, are very, very sick, and many are very, very unhappy and die young. It's obvious that we need more understanding of this great commitment to us by our Father through His Word, so that we can act according to its rules.

Now in this that I declare unto you I praise you not, that ye come together not for the better, but for the worse.

For first of all, when ye come together in the church, I hear that there be divisions among you; and I partly believe it.

For there must be also heresies among you, that they which are approved may be made manifest among you.

When ye come together therefore in one place, this is not to eat the Lord's supper.

For in eating every one taketh before other his own supper: and one is hungry, and another is drunken.

What? have ye not houses to eat and drink in? or despise ye the church of God, and shame them that have not? What shall I say to you? shall I praise you in this? I praise you not.

For I have received of the Lord that which also I delivered unto you, That the Lord Jesus the same night in which he was betrayed took bread:

And when he had given thanks, he brake it, and said, Take, eat: this is my body, which is broken for you: this do in remembrance of me.

For as often as ye eat this bread, and drink this cup, ye do shew the Lord's death till he come.

Wherefore whosoever shall eat this bread, and drink this cup of the Lord, unworthily, shall be guilty of the body and blood of the Lord.

But let a man examine himself, and so let him eat of that bread, and drink of that cup.

For he that eateth and drinketh unworthily, eateth and drinketh damnation to himself, not discerning the Lord's body.

For this cause many are weak and sickly among you, and many sleep.

For if we would judge ourselves, we should not be judged.

But when we are judged, we are chastened of the Lord, that we should not be condemned with the world.

Wherefore, my brethren, when ye come together to eat, tarry one for another.

And if any man hunger, let him eat at home; that ye come not together unto condemnation. And the rest will I set in order when I come.

1 Corinthians 11:17-34

The reason this wonderful sacrament is in an epistle of Paul's that deals with prayer is that it is one of the very greatest commitments, with promise, that God ever made to His people. Therefore, whether it is a prayer or a promise, the rules must be known and followed for lasting benefits to be received.

Paul addresses the Corinthian church on this subject with more anger in his words than on any other subject he addresses to the churches in all of his letters to them. You can hear him say, "Don't you know any better? What are you doing? Are you dull? You would be better off to stay home. You *are much worse off* by taking communion in the way you are doing it. You would be *better off* not to take it at all than the way you're doing it."

Why is the apostle so angry? Is it because there are divisions and cliques? Is it because they are gluttons? No. These things could be prevalent in any church. Why then is he writing such a strong admonition in such terms of rebuke? Please notice verse 22 where the word *despise* is used. Most Greek scholars know you could substitute the word "hate" here. The Corinthians actually were acting in such a way that showed *no respect* for God's house, or the place set aside for *worship* unto Him. Both reverence and knowledge are missing. It's not just lack of respect for a house, but a lack of respect for the act of Holy Communion. This letter written by the apostle addresses the significant subject of the suffering and death of Jesus.

Their lack of commitment to physical discipline surfaces in how they ate and drank. This lack also will surface in us, if we allow it do so. It will follow us into our entire spiritual life. Are we any different today? Even though we may not gorge ourselves with food just before we take communion, we must admit that the 20th century church is not as physically disciplined as it ought to be, nor do we seem to understand communion any better than they did.

Warnings Against Unworthy Partaking

After the Apostle gives the instruction for partaking of communion in verses 24-26, he proceeds to give one of the strongest warnings he could give to those who partake in an *unworthy* manner. Those people would be as guilty as the ones who actually drove the nails into the hands of the Lord, as guilty as Pilate, or the Jews who gave Him to the Roman soldiers to be crucified. To partake of communion without respect or knowledge not only puts one in a criminal category but leads to sickness which, in turn, leads to premature death.

The word *unworthily* has been misunderstood grossly. As a result, certain churches have strict rules that are prohibitive to those who should be partaking. In some denominational churches, they have what they call "closed communion." Although you are a Christian and happen to visit their church on communion Sunday, you will not be served unless you are a member of that particular church, not even if you belong to a church of the same denomination in a different location. In some countries, Christians will not be served communion by the missionaries if they have not been tithing. Many more breaches of the teaching on communion could be mentioned. They are very serious breaches.

The word *unworthily* can be understood only by using it in connection with the phrase in the last part of verse 29, **not discerning the Lord's body,** or not understanding what really happened when Jesus died. While there is, in this entire context, a good teaching against gluttony, cliques and divisions, strife, and doing disrespectful things — especially in the exercise of the sacrament, these are not the heart of the abuse which Paul addresses.

We should judge our behavior lest we be judged, but the act of saying, "You should not take communion if you are not where you ought to be in the Lord," misses the whole purpose of Christ's death and the very reason we are to partake of the communion service. He died, He shed His blood, gave His all to take upon Himself our sins and diseases. This is what communion is all about. He did all this so we could become His righteousness as we receive His sacrificial death in our stead.

Adam Clarke expresses it so well concerning the eating and drinking of the Lord's Supper and this admonition: **Whosoever shall eat...and drink...unworthily.** He concludes, "To put a final end to controversies and perplexities relative to these words and the context, let the reader observe, that to eat and drink the bread and wine in the Lord's Supper unworthily, is to eat and drink as the Corinthians did, who ate it not in reference to *Jesus Christ's sacrificial death*; but rather in such a way as the Israelites did the Passover, which they celebrated in remembrance of their deliverance from the Egyptian bondage.

"Likewise, these mongrel Christians at Corinth used it as a kind of historical commemoration of the death of Christ; and did not, in the whole institution, discern the Lord's body and blood as a sacrificial offering for sin; and besides, in their celebration of it they acted in a way utterly unbecoming the gravity of a sacred ordinance. Those who *acknowledge* it as a *sacrificial offering,* and receive it in remembrance of God's love to them in sending His Son into the world, can neither bring damnation upon themselves by so doing, nor eat nor drink unworthily."[1] (Italicized emphasis added by the author.)

Traditional Warnings Miss the Mark

The normal approach in most Protestant churches is the traditional approach, with the traditional warnings which focus on the *partaker* rather than on the *elements* themselves. You might hear the pastor say, "Please do not partake of these elements if you have sin in your life," or, as already noted previously, "If you have not paid your tithes," or "If you are not a member of this church." While we will always need spiritual admonitions for the believer to examine himself, to do so at communion time is to take away from the efficacy of the cross and the sacrifice of our Savior.

Would it not be much, much better to simply say, "All are welcome to approach the sacraments. Jesus, our Lord, died for all, shed His blood for all sins, great and small. If you have failed, then partake with full understanding of what your Lord Jesus did for you in His suffering for your sins. Forgiveness is for you. Rest assured that the sin question is settled. Salvation is assured. Eat all of it, and drink all of it, and go forth to sin no more."

The Rev. Jack Hayford, pastor of Church on the Way in Los Angeles, in a sermon given in a conference in Panama some years ago, drew attention to the Greek word, *axios*, translated "worthy." He discovered, in his study on the word, that it was used also of coins that had to be weighed to see if they had lost any of their worth by constant use. (See W. E. Vine's.) To approach the communion table thinking about your *own* worth is to do exactly the opposite of what is intended. You, your failure and faults, need not be constantly dealt with. Here we are dealing with the subject of what Jesus is, what He did, and what He can do now. It is *His worth* that needs to be considered, not ours. Note the key phrase, **Not discerning the Lord's body,** meaning "not understanding what the communion table and sacraments are all about."

There is another great and awesome warning in Luke 22:22. Here Jesus is partaking of the Last Supper with His disciples. After He gives the instruction, and they partake, Jesus says, **and truly the Son of man goeth, as it was determined: but woe unto that man by whom he is betrayed!** Judas did not ever fully understand who Jesus was, nor what He came to do. He misjudged the Lord and His mission completely. He allowed his own weakness, love of money and of self, to blank out of his mind, his thought, and his understanding, the coming death of Jesus. He allowed these sins to cause him to betray Jesus. Judas turned inward to self-service, thinking only of what was in it for him, instead of turning his attention outward to Jesus where it should have been.

The Apostle Paul literally, as we would say in the vernacular today, "jumped all over" the carnal, selfish, gluttonous, drinking Corinthians for the same failure.

They were failing to discern for what purpose Jesus came, what His death and resurrection were all about. They were turned inward instead of outward. Inward to the flesh instead of outward to the cross, which was their only hope.

No wonder that, for this cause, many of them were weak and sickly (as many more are today), the opposite of strong . . . *and many of you sleep, or die.* If we judge ourselves, we will not be judged. This judgment of sickness and death is the result (even as it was on Judas Iscariot) of not understanding, not discerning what Jesus came to do. This is why we partake of the elements to remind us, not of our failures, sins, and shortcomings, but to remind us that our Lord Jesus gave His body and shed His blood so that we could be free from sin and sickness and live unto righteousness.

A Word to Pastors

Many, many people should be healed as they partake, and some should even be saved or reclaimed. Pastors, please don't heap condemnation on the sheep as they partake, but minister truth to them that will set them free. Don't call attention to the partaker and his faults, but focus all the attention on the elements that represent what Jesus came to accomplish.

By calling attention to our own weaknesses, we discourage the celebration of what our Lord Jesus died to accomplish. Prohibiting someone from partaking because his name is not on the church roll is not only wrong but very close to doing exactly opposite of what should be done! The same is true when a pastor says, "Do not partake if there is sin in your life." This is the very time when the sacrament is most needed. This is the time when the partaker needs to understand what it is that Jesus did for him.

Pastors, communion offers the greatest arena in which to call attention to the finished work of the cross. It is a paramount time of importance to make all present understand salvation and healing in that work. Call attention to Jesus. Lift up and exalt Him. Do not focus in on our failures — but on His victory!

---

[1] Adam Clarke, *Commentary on the Entire Bible* (Grand Rapids: Baker Books, 1967).

10
RULES: INTERCESSION

Intercessional prayer has experienced a greater emphasis in the past five years than for the past century. The word itself simply means "to go to someone on behalf of another." In Greek usage, it means the same. The Greek noun *enteuxis*, means "to light upon, petition." It is translated "prayer" in 1 Timothy 4:5, but in 1 Timothy 2:1, it is translated "intercessions." The Greek verb *entugchano*, primarily means "to fall in with, to make petition," especially "to make intercession, to plead with a person either for or against others." In Romans 8:27, it is used of the intercessional work of the Holy Spirit for the saints.

> If my people, which are called by my name, shall humble themselves, and pray, and seek my face, and turn from their wicked ways; then will I hear from heaven, and will forgive their sin, and will heal their land.
>
> 2 Chronicles 7:14

I will address the act of prayer later, but now a greater need of clarity has arisen, and that is, "Are intercessors an elect group, set apart and above many others? Is intercession only for a few select, or is it something for all saints to know about and take part in? Are we all to be intercessors? Have we made a big mistake in allowing a few saints to be called intercessors?"

The rules for this great exercise should have been laid down many years ago. Some damage already has been experienced by the Church's failure to do so. Paul taught us in 1 Timothy 2:1-3.

> I exhort therefore, that, first of all, supplications, prayers, intercessions, and giving of thanks, be made for all men;
>
> For kings, and for all that are in authority; that we may lead a quiet and peaceable life in all godliness and honesty.
>
> For this is good and acceptable in the sight of God our Saviour.

The Apostle Paul, in the above admonition, urges *all* to be a participant in intercession. Not only is it a *command*, but a *performance*, a *carrying out*, of this act we are to do *first* each day. Notice the writer's use of four words in this approach to God in prayer.

Four Important Words on Intercession

1. **Supplications:** The Greek word *deesis* does not add anything to the English. Adam Clarke's commentary calls it "prayers for averting evils of every kind." We may all be sure the apostle meant more than a casual prayer when he used this word here as he also used it in connection with the word *prayer* in his other epistles. I especially like the way Clarke calls attention to the fact that we come against evil of every kind when we make supplications.

2. **Prayers:** This is to be first, every day, going to God in Jesus' name and praying for our rulers. It is a powerful concept. This is something I do first every day. I not only pray as instructed by Paul, but mention the

name of the President of the United States. I am sure many do this also, but do they do it *before* they pray for family or friends? Again, Adam Clarke believed it was referring to prayers for obtaining the good things, spiritual and temporal, which we, ourselves, also need.

3. **Intercessions:** As we mentioned before, this is going to one on behalf of another.

4. **Giving of thanks:** This phase has not only been overlooked here, but greatly neglected in general by all saints. Why be faithful to make supplication, prayers, and intercessions, and then leave this great truth out of the total picture?

Let a family scene give you a clearer picture. Johnny and Susie come to Mother with the well-known supplication — prayer, request, intercession, pleading — for whatever they need at that moment. As usual, they get their request and out the door they go with whatever it was they wanted, letting it slam as usual — not a backward look, not a heartfelt "Thank you," not an "I love you, Mom," or "You're the greatest." If you were surveying that scene, you would probably remark, "What they really need is not the answer to their request, but a good paddling, and then some denial until they learn to appreciate what has been done for them." Perhaps our Heavenly Father should deal with us in this same way when we are unappreciative.

Most importantly, it is to be noticed that verse 3 of 1 Timothy 2 states: **For such [praying] is good and right, and [it is] pleasing and acceptable to God our Savior** (AMP). *All,* not a few, are to be intercessors. *All* are to remember those in authority over them. *All* are to come against the evil of the day. *All* are to continually be giving thanks. What is the end of such praying? That *all* would enjoy a quiet and peaceable life in all godliness and honesty.

What great proof that all of God's saints are to be intercessors. *All* are to pray. *All* are to live in peace. If *all* do not pray, then *all* are not going to live in peace and comfort in the land wherever they live. Speaking of lands and countries that need such prayers reminds us of the Israelites and God's promise to them. They were told by their God to humble themselves and pray. In that admonition, we have the perfect rules laid down that adequately describe the qualifications of an intercessor. *If* again. That little word is not only a qualifying word, but *if* the rules are not met, the rest of the verse is void or does not apply.

Many religions have millions of people who pray more often than we do. Some even pray five times a day. They will pray in a moving train or vehicle, an airplane, or a busy street. But their prayers will go unanswered, if they are not His people. We must be people *called by His name, known by His name.* It is important to be known by all to be people associated with His name and identified with His holiness. Church affiliation is secondary.

No Humility Without Submission

The word *humility* in 2 Chronicles 7:14 is as big a word in meaning as the little word *if.* Those who want their prayer heard and answered, and especially those who call themselves intercessors, must resist any tendencies of pride over good things that happen as a result of their praying. Intercessors are not above the pastor. They are not to think of themselves as some elite group. They must be, as all of us must be, very humble before their God. There is no true humility without true submission.

Likewise, ye younger, submit yourselves unto the elder. Yea, all of you be subject one to another, and be clothed with humility: for God resisteth the proud, and giveth grace to the humble.

1 Peter 5:5

As God began to call the Church's attention to, and emphasize, the need for intercessors prior to the coming great outpouring, many responded favorably. In fact, some good and faithful servants and hand-maidens crisscrossed our nation conducting intercessors' seminars. This was all good and had good results. One negative thing surfaced, however, through no fault of those holding the seminars, and that was a tendency toward pride in some that attended. I trust, and believe, that this has been dealt with, and there are many still responding to this call for intercessors.

Pastors should be calling days of fasting and prayer for their entire congregations and not relying on just a few to make intercession for the many. Remember, 2 Chronicles 7:14 is a call to prayer for *all* of God's people and not just a few here and there.

Please note that there is a difference in praying and seeking God's face. God cannot heal the land and the home and bless an entire nation on prayer alone. The seeking of God's face suggests a personal desire for each prayer to draw close to God, to have personal commitment and holiness in his walk with the Lord.

I hear pastors say, "My people are a praying people." But nothing is happening in their churches. Why is this? Prayer *alone* is not enough to bring revival and blessing. God cannot bless sin. He cannot overlook rebellion, gossip, unforgiveness, and criticism. His face must be sought. *Seek* also means "to put first." God must be first in the lives of His people, or there will not be revival. God cannot ignore sin. There must be a turning from the wicked ways, a turning from worldliness.

So many of our Pentecostal people are more and more becoming movie fans or sports enthusiasts and are becoming caught up in entertainment. We see more and more satellite dishes that bring the immorality and sexual perverseness that is so predominant in the entertainment world right into our living rooms and bedrooms. Remember, pastor; remember, Church; no blessing of His is poured out until wicked ways are forsaken.

A good shepherd will know that part of his assignment is to so minister so that his sheep will hate sin and love the sinner. We are fast approaching the day when dispensations will once again be overlapping as when Jesus came to fulfill the law. But while He yet lived on earth, the law was in force. Jesus died and rose again, but the Church Age did not begin until the Day of Pentecost was fully come.

We are now very near the end of the Church Age and very, very close to the millennium, that perfect age that will be free from sickness and death and Satan. Here is a word for those of you who pray. It is from a millennium setting in Isaiah 65:24.

And it shall come to pass, that before they call, I will answer; and while they are yet speaking, I will hear.

This is going to happen to some people during the overlapping of the Church's day and the perfect reign of Christ in person. Believe it will happen to you as you seek God's face, as you humble yourself and pray, turning from your wicked ways. Even as you are in that time of intercession, in that very act, God is answering and revival is flowing.

The phone may ring while you are on your knees and, even before you begin to pray, the answer may come. Take courage, prayer warrior; take courage, intercessor. Keep the vigils. Keep on using your prayer language, even stammering lips that may not sound like any language you have ever heard. (Is. 28:11.) To further make the point that a believer, baptized with the Holy Spirit, can make intercession and that it is not limited to a few, look at Romans 8:26,27.

Likewise the Spirit also helpeth our infirmities: for we know not what we should pray for as we ought: but the Spirit itself maketh intercession for us with groanings which cannot be uttered.

And he that searcheth the hearts knoweth what is the mind of the Spirit, because he maketh intercession for the saints according to the will of God.

It is true that the Holy Spirit of God helps us as we enter into intercession. But it is also true that we must initiate the action. Dr. T. J. McCrossan in his book, *Bodily Healing and the Atonement*,[1] states that the Greek word for *helpeth* means "to take hold against together with." If we believers, baptized in the Holy Spirit, desire to enter into intercession, we must begin to speak with tongues first. Then the Holy Spirit takes hold together with us against the work of the enemy. He apparently cannot, and does not, pray to God on His own or for Himself, but only as we initiate the action ourselves. We do not know how to pray as we ought, but the Third Person of the Trinity knows what is the mind of God and what is the will of God, thus praying with tongues assures us that we have not wasted a word.

I like *The New English Bible* version of the last part of Romans 8:26, . . . **but through our inarticulate groans the Spirit himself is pleading for us.**[2]

Reader, please do not allow anyone who opposes speaking with tongues to rob you of this great truth. True intercession is allowing the true Intercessor to pray through you.

Prayer

And now, my Father, that I know the rules for intercessory prayer, please help me to initiate that action of faith that will allow Your precious Holy Spirit in me to make intercession for me, for the Church, and for the sinner. I believe You hear me, thus I will act accordingly. In Jesus' name. Amen.

---

[1] Dr. T. J. McCrossan, *Bodily Healing and the Atonement*, re-edited by Dr. Roy H. Hicks and Dr. Kenneth Hagin (Tulsa: Rhema Bible Church, 1982).

[2] *The New English Bible* (London: Collins World, 1961, 1970).

11
RULES: ROMANS 8:28, PHILIPPIANS 4:19, 3 JOHN 2

Romans 8:28 is one of the most frequently used and precious promises in the New Testament. It is often quoted to a child of God who may have had an exceptional setback. It could be a sudden loss of what was considered to be secure employment or a tragic accident that caused the severe maiming or death of a loved one or a breach in what was considered by all to be a very loving marriage. Too many times it turns out to be unexpected rebellion in a child of a family everyone thought was really happy.

It is during these occasions that we frequently hear this precious promise quoted. It is quoted in good faith, received in good faith, and produces a great sense of expectancy — and well it should. But, alas, the promise is very seldom experienced as it should be. We all know this, but tend to ignore the symptoms in those who do not seem to be receiving the "good" this promise should produce.

And we know that all things work together for good to them that love God, to them who are the called according to his purpose.

Being in the ministry for many years, both as pastor of a church and later a "pastor of pastors" in the office of bishop, I can personally cite many, many tragic incidents and accidents where the good was not forth-coming as was expected. May this chapter not take away from anyone, even in a small way, the hope this verse *can* bring. My desire is to be honest and not busy our pen in the proverbial "theological sand." But this verse, with the high hope it generates, will not work — cannot work — unless understood and conceived correctly as one stands upon it.

The first time I became aware of the Greek tenses in this verse was while reading Adam Clarke's commentary. He says, "That the persons in whose behalf all things work for good are they who love God, and consequently, who live in the spirit of obedience. It is not said that all things shall work for good, but that they work *now* in the behalf of him who *loveth now;* for both verbs are in the present tense." He goes on to say, "They who say sin works for good to them that love God speak blasphemous nonsense."[1]

It is not my desire to be judgmental. It is my desire to encourage you to understand what God is saying and to encourage you to love God *now*, present tense, and to keep on loving God every day.

We must not forget, however, that our individual love of God cannot cover another loved one's rebellion. If that were so, no one could ever suffer any ill. God never promised us that our children would be imper-vious to Satan's temptation. He never said anywhere in His Word that temptation would not come near us. He did promise us that we, personally, by loving Him every day, would be kept, and that we can cast our care upon Him.

If, for instance, one has a wayward child, living in sin, the only way that can work out for our personal good is for that child to come back to Him. (See Jeremiah 31:16,17.) If we are to be free of darkness, sorrow, and grief, we must believe Romans 8:28, cast our care upon Jesus, and sleep in peace. The same would apply to a spouse that left, remarried, and had children. That situation cannot work for good unless it is cast completely on our Lord. This means the injured party must stop talking about the harm and hurt that was done and stop feeling rejected and getting into self-pity. It doesn't mean the first marriage will be restored.

If the injured party fulfills the conditions, then for that one, all things will work together for the good expected, although maybe not in the way expected. Please notice that this promise is not only to those who love God but to those who love God *and* also are serving and called to His purposes. So many times we attempt to quote this great promise and apply it to those who not only were not loving Him at the particular time of their difficulty but also were not obeying the call to serve God's purposes and His will for their lives. Or perhaps the injured party was, but the other person involved was not.

This calling, or invitation, is the same as being invited to sit with kings and princes in a festive setting. So the verse is for those who love God now and, in addition, are being obedient servants. They are not merely obeying, but obeying with joy. Please, reader, learn carefully the rules for this great verse. Apply them and reap its great blessings.

Preciseness for Precious Promises

Another great verse that is quoted almost as much as Romans 8:28 is Philippians 4:19: **But my God shall supply all your need according to his riches in glory by Christ Jesus.**

I have heard it, in my 42 years of ministry, quoted under all circumstances more than any other verse in the Bible. I know of no one in gospel work who has ever disagreed on the context of this often-quoted promise. All seem to agree that it is quoted completely out of context, yet everyone seems reluctant to correct its misapplication. Please forgive me for being blunt and right to the point — it should have been done long ago.

First, please note that Paul did not quote this promise for himself. There is no evidence that he did, at all times and under every circumstance, have all his needs met. It is very clear that, at times, he had to work with his hands. Some of the churches he pioneered failed to support him. (Phil. 4:15.) Paul refers to his times of need as "afflictions." (Phil. 4:15.)

This fourth chapter of Philippians supports the teaching of 2 Corinthians 8. Paul literally is giving the same teaching. In 2 Corinthians 8:7, Paul admonishes the saints to abound in their ministry of giving. If they were obedient in giving, then their own need would be met. (2 Cor. 8:14.)

This great promise belongs to all saints of all times. It is based entirely on giving. We will have our need supplied *if* we are faithful and obedient to give. There is not one shred of truth or hope that God will supply the need of anyone who is not already giving in abundance. In his letters both to the assemblies at Corinth and at Philippi, Paul made it clear that the need of Christians would not be met unless they continued to give to the poor saints and to the ministry of the workers, as well.

Paul is not addressing tithing. He is not speaking of any support for the local church and its ministries. I have known many pastors who used 2 Corinthians 8 and Philippians 4 in an endeavor to prove that tithing is not a New Testament principle. Tithing didn't originate under the law, but under grace with Abraham. Jesus was very outspoken on the subject of which laws He did not want to see continue. So it is significant that He did not at any time touch the tithing principle that began under Abraham. It continued under the disciples and the early Church even to this present day.

Jesus taught giving as a means to receiving. (Luke 6:38.) Paul does the same in Philippians 4:15. "Give to the ministry above your tithe. Give to the poor saints, give to missionaries, and then **My God shall supply all your need according to his riches in glory by Christ Jesus."**

The Prosperity Promise

Third John 2 is one promise that has to be everyone's favorite! If it isn't, they must be unaware of John's prayer for all saints.

Beloved, I wish above all things that thou mayest prosper and be in health, even as thy soul prospereth.

Those individuals who teach against the message of health and prosperity in God's Word, saying, "It is

93

not for today," are either saying that John wrote that thought to Gaius alone, or they are saying that health and prosperity were to end with that generation! It is almost ludicrous. If that were true, they would have to use the same argument for being born again, because Jesus most certainly was talking to Nicodemus alone. Yet He knew that His words would be written down for all future generations to read and appropriate the same principle for their lives.

Adam Clarke says in his commentary written 150 years ago: "These three things, so necessary to the comfort of life, every Christian may in a certain measure expect, and for them every Christian is authorized to pray; and we should have more of all three if we devoutly prayed for them."[2]

Guidelines Anyone Can Apply

Following are four guidelines that anyone can ask himself or herself and can apply to any of the promises:

1. To whom does the promise apply?

2. Does it apply to me personally?

3. Are there any conditions involved? If so, what are they?

4. Am I committed to "following through" on the conditions?

In this third letter of John's, he was writing to a beloved brother, a Christian who had been faithful in hospitality with a spirit of giving. He was greatly loved and respected by the total Body of Christ. He had met all of the conditions, thus John's wish for him. This great promise, which can be appropriated by all saints, can be yours as you continue in love and have a spirit of liberality.

Now you know God's attitude toward your finances, your physical health, and your soul. God's first emphasis is on your soul — may it be prosperous. A prosperous soul is a well-fed soul, one that is fed on the Word of God. The mind is full of the Word of God, so that you can meditate upon it. You are fellowshipping, in harmony with the saints. You are well-received by God's people. Now you can claim prosperity for your finances and physical and mental health.

Remember that financial prosperity simply means having all of your personal needs met and having something left over to give to others. God's health frees you to pursue your calling. The economy of the world flows and flourishes by investments in its market programs. God's economy works the same. The only difference is that we invest in God's programs and His people. Yes, you give to get. You invest to receive. There is nothing wrong in teaching that you give to get, as long as you give again! Be sure that your motive is God's harvest and not your own, and God's blessing will flow to you.

Prayer

Dear Father, I desire to be a beloved Christian like Gaius. I desire to be given to hospitality and to be a generous giver. I desire to be in good health, and I claim this promise for me and my loved ones. Please help me to be such an outstanding child of Yours that all saints will call me beloved as they witness the prosperity of my soul. In the name of Jesus, Your son.

---

[1] Adam Clarke, *Commentary on the Entire Bible* (Grand Rapids: Baker Books, n.d.).

[2] *Ibid.*

12

RULES: THE PRAYER FOR
UNSAVED FAMILY MEMBERS

The Word makes it very clear that our Father is a family God. He loves the family and does not want to see any member of your family lost. He does not want to see any of His children unhappy. Seeing an unsaved spouse or child or family member under your direct influence continually reject Jesus and continue in sin is very painful and causes weeping and sorrow. One of the many scriptures you can stand on for your family's salvation is Acts 16:31 (AMP).

> **And they answered, Believe in *and* on the Lord Jesus *Christ* — that is, give yourself up to Him, take yourself out of your own keeping and entrust yourself into His keeping, and you will be saved; [and this applies both to] you and your household as well.**

While we can fully understand and appreciate God's concern and will for our family, we must also equate that with another great irreversible truth: God will not go against your loved one's personal will. Definitely, there will be no one in heaven against his or her will! No one will be going around sowing seeds of discord and unhappiness because they did not choose to be there. The great truths of the Bible are only applicable when a person receives Jesus as Savior and remains *in* Christ.

To receive Christ at one point and time in your life does not, and cannot, ever mean you lose any control of your own will. You not only retain your will, but you can change your will and turn back again to your former lifestyle, even as a pig returns to its wallowing in the mud and as a dog to its vomit. (2 Pet. 2:22.) A Christian is secure as long as he abides in Christ Jesus, but it is plainly shown in the Bible that a Christian does keep his own will even when setting his will to do the Lord's will. It is still the Christian's own choice.

This, then, brings to the surface a very, very important point. If my unsaved family member is willfully rejecting Christ and serving sin, how can God answer my prayer without going against that person's will? The answer, of course, is that He does *not* go against that person's will. Through my prayers and my standing on the Word of God, the will of that unsaved loved one can be changed to come in line with the will of God.

How to Change the Will of an Unsaved Person

There is only one way to change the will of anyone: by causing that person to change his or her mind. The only way to change someone's mind where God is concerned is to reach that person with God's Word, either in the natural through another human being or in the supernatural through the Holy Spirit's wooing of the spirit of that person. Several prayers are involved here — *claiming that person for God, the prayer of intercession in the Spirit, the prayer of thanksgiving for that person's salvation, and the prayer for laborers to be sent across his or her path.* Some examples of these kinds of prayers are at the end of this chapter. Also, the devil's work in that person's life can be bound.

The best prayers are those which involve the double-edged sword of the Lord: His own Word already given in the Bible. There are many verses listed throughout this chapter that can be used. Other verses can be found through a good concordance or a Bible that includes such helps. Once you have prayed and claimed that person's salvation, the next step is to intercede for that person until you have a peace in your heart that the work is done.

> Likewise the Spirit also helpeth our infirmities: for we know not what we should pray for as we ought: but the Spirit itself maketh intercession for us with groanings which cannot be uttered.
>
> And he that searcheth the hearts knoweth what is the mind of the Spirit, because he maketh intercession for the saints according to the will of God.
>
> **Romans 8:26,27**

Intercession involves spiritual warfare to break the bondages of any possible satanic influence. Any satanic power in that life should be broken.

Because this person is unsaved, he or she is unable to understand the things of God. Witnessing to them is fine — *if* you do not become so "pushy" that you push them further away as a reaction to you. The best way to witness to anyone usually is to show the fruit of the Holy Spirit (Gal. 5:22-24) in your own life and allow that person to see the love of Jesus in and through you. Many times, the mind of a family member is blinded and even antagonistic to the things of God.

But if our gospel be hid, it is hid to them that are lost:

In whom the god of this world hath blinded the minds of them which believe not, lest the light of the glorious gospel of Christ, who is the image of God, should shine unto them.

2 Corinthians 4:3,4

If this is the case with the person for whom you are concerned, the power that Jesus gave believers over all the power of the enemy needs to be exercised in spiritual warfare. We do not have authority over anyone else's will, but we *do* have authority over satanic influences.

Ye are of God, little children, and have overcome them: because greater is he that is in you, than he that is in the world.

1 John 4:4

Behold, I give unto you power to tread on serpents and scorpions, and over all the power of the enemy: and nothing shall by any means hurt you.

Luke 10:19

Verily I say unto you, Whatsoever ye shall bind on earth shall be bound in heaven: and whatsoever ye shall loose on earth shall be loosed in heaven.

Matthew 18:18

According to these scriptures, *in the name and authority of Jesus,* we can bind the works of the devil in the lives of our spouses, children, or family members under our headship. One important thing to remember, however, is that you have to understand this authority and believe that you have it. Otherwise, your words will be no better than those spoken in a namby-pamby way to a dog. That dog will just look at you and not move. The power is in the name of Jesus, but the authority comes through your will and voice.

When you have claimed a family member, bound the power of the devil in his or her life, and interceded until you have a witness that it is done, then thank the Lord for their salvation — and keep thanking Him until it is manifested in the natural world. This is the time to stand in faith on God's Word.

> And this is the confidence that we have in him, that, if we ask any thing according to his will, he heareth us:
>
> And if we know that he hear us, whatsoever we ask, we know that we have the petitions that we desired of him.
>
> 1 John 5:14,15

> ...having done all, to stand.
>
> Ephesians 6:13

While you are *standing* on God's Word knowing it is His will for this person to be saved and knowing that you have done all that you can do to bring that about, there is one more thing that can be done: the sending of laborers across his or her path.

> How then shall they call on him in whom they have not believed? and how shall they believe in him of whom they have not heard? and how shall they hear without a preacher?
>
> So then faith cometh by hearing, and hearing by the word of God.
>
> Romans 10:14,17

> Therefore said he unto them, The harvest truly is great, but the labourers are few: pray ye therefore the Lord

of the harvest, that he would send forth labourers into his harvest.

Luke 10:2

You can pray that God will cause other Christians to cross the paths of that loved one and plant or water or bring to harvest the seed of the Word in that life. Confess Matthew 13:3,8 and believe that good seed of the Word is bringing fruit in the life of your family member.

The Urgency of This Generation

Looking back into history when there was age after age and generation following generation with few cultural and religious changes, there was not always the sense of urgency over unsaved loved ones that we have today. We, above all past generations, face a very different challenge — to get our loved ones into God's family before the Rapture.

Living in the end times, we face this glorious experience at any moment. In the past, unsaved loved ones, even those who were as hard-hearted as some today, hopefully would repent on their deathbed, if not before. People remained conscious right up to the moment of death in most cases, unlike the situation today with anesthetics and modern hospital techniques. God had that much time to work with them. At the resurrection, time will cease suddenly and forever. There will be no time for repentance or prayer. Also, in our high-technology lifestyle, there are many more chances for sudden death than there were in past ages.

We face the possibility that there is a strong chance our unsaved loved ones will not have the time to repent that others before us had. The Rapture *will* take place in a moment, in the twinkling of an eye, even faster than the speed of light. (1 Cor. 15:52.) There will not even be a second to say, "Save me, Lord." Those left behind will hear nothing, see nothing, feel nothing, as we leave.

This thought of not having time to repent if Jesus comes prompted me to write this chapter of the rules for the promises of God. We who have unsaved loved ones should realize this possible situation and go to the Bible to find out if there is any teaching as to what to do in such drastic circumstances. There are many verses on which to stand in prayer for the salvation of all the members of your own immediate family.

In a previous book, *Another Look at the Rapture,*[1] I dealt with some of the following verses. I encourage you to look them up, repeat them daily, and believe them whole-heartedly: Jeremiah 31:16,17; Jeremiah 30:20; Joel 2:32; Matthew 18:14; Luke 19:10; John 20:31; and Acts 16:31. Remember, effective prayer means taking into God's presence His own Words.

Our Father, God, has great compassion for the family. He does not want to see one member saved and another lost. He is a family-loving God.

If the child, or other family member, for whom you are concerned was reared in the way of the Lord but seems to be wandering away as did the Prodigal Son, this verse originally written to Israel can be spiritually applied to your situation. Claim and stand on this verse for the returning of that person to the Lord:

> **Thus saith the Lord; Restrain thy voice from weeping, and thine eyes from tears; for thy work shall be**

rewarded, saith the Lord, and they shall come again from the land of the enemy.

And there is hope in thine end, saith the Lord, that thy children shall come again to their own border.

Jeremiah 31:16,17

Prayer Claiming Salvation of a Family Member

Dear Lord Jesus, Head of the Church, we come to ask You to give us help. You alone can look ahead and know if my loved one (insert the person's name here) *will be saved and ready to meet You when You come for Your church, or when* (name) *dies and goes to meet You. If, Lord Jesus, You see that* (name) *will not be ready, please do whatever it takes to get him or her ready.*

I do not want to see this person suffer, yet it would be better to suffer here under conviction for a short time than physically in hell for all eternity.

I thank You that Your Word in Acts 16:31 promises me that, if I will believe on You, not only will I be saved but all the members of my household. I thank You that You keep Your Word, and I now enter into agreement with You and commit (name) *to Your care. I am trusting the dear Holy Spirit to do His work, and I believe I will see* (name) *in Heaven. Amen.*

Statement of Binding and Loosing

You satanic spirit, in the name of Jesus Christ, I bind you from hindering (insert person's name) *from receiving the Word of God. You spirit of rebellion, I bind you from hardening* (his or her) *heart to the Lord and from blinding* (his or her) *eyes to the truth.*

Any spirits of Satan that are involved with this person, I now loose you from your assignments in the name of Jesus and bind you from interfering again in this life.

I command you spirits now to loose your grip on (name) and break your power over (name) in Jesus' name.

Prayer for Laborers

Dear Heavenly Father, Jesus said for us to pray for You to send out laborers into the field to bring in the harvest. Now, Father, I ask You, in accordance with Your Word, to send laborers across the path of (insert name). You know best which one of Your servants can touch the heart and mind of (name) and is available to minister to (name). And I ask You now to send that one whom You know is able through the Holy Spirit to bring in the harvest of my family member. I thank You, Lord, for Your Word, for Your promises, for Your love for me and my family, and for Your faithfulness to perform that which You have said. Amen.

Prayer of Thanksgiving for Salvation

I thank You, Lord, that the eyes of (insert person's name) *are being opened to the truth of Your Word. I thank You that my prayers are being answered. I thank You for the salvation of* (name). *I thank You that You are moving in the life of* (name) *right now! I thank You that it is done.*

---

[1] Roy H. Hicks, *Another Look at the Rapture* (Tulsa: Harrison House, 1982).

Books by Dr. Roy H. Hicks

Obtaining Promises
A Different Approach for Every Promise

Keys of the Kingdom

Instrument Rated Christian

Healing Your Insecurities

Praying Beyond God's Ability
Why Prayers Go Unanswered

Use It Or Lose It
The Word of Faith

He Who Laughs Lasts . . . And Lasts . . . And Lasts

Another Look At The Rapture

The Power of Positive Resistance
The Christian's Antihistamine

Whatever Happened to Hope?

Available from your local bookstore.

Harrison House

P. O. Box 35035 • Tulsa, Oklahoma 74153

Roy H. Hicks is a successful minister of the Gospel who has given his life to pastoring and pioneering churches throughout the United States. He has served the Lord in various foreign fields, having made missionary journeys to South America, the Orient, Australia, and New Zealand.

Dr. Hicks formerly served as General Supervisor of the Foursquare Gospel Churches and has become a popular speaker at charismatic conferences.

Perhaps the thing that most endears Dr. Hicks to readers is his warmth and his ability to reach out as the true believer he is — a man of strong, positive faith, sharing a refreshing ministry through the power and anointing of the Holy Spirit.

To contact Dr. Hicks,
write:

Dr. Roy H. Hicks
P. O. Box 4113
San Marcos, California 92069

*Please include your prayer requests
and comments when you write.*